Believe in Better

"In *Believe in Better*, Damon Stafford provides leadership principles that have been developed through the highs and lows of his remarkable journey as an entrepreneur. This book delivers inspiring and universal strategies in relatable, experience-driven, and humorous ways. In my career, I have advised hundreds of business owners and executives across a wide variety of industries. Damon's principles are relevant and valuable to any leader regardless of career stage, industry, or size of company."

Phil Colaço
Retired CEO, Deloitte Corporate Finance; Retired Global Leader, Deloitte Corporate Finance Advisory

"As someone who has spent decades helping companies scale up, I can say with confidence that the principles Damon shares are the very essence of what it takes to build not just a successful business, but a sustainable one. From fostering a culture of transparency to embracing change as a constant, *Believe in Better* is a clarion call to leaders and entrepreneurs to never settle for being the best. They need to be better."

Verne Harnish
Founder, Entrepreneurs' Organization (EO); Author, Scaling Up (Rockefeller Habits 2.0)

"What sets *Believe in Better* apart is its raw honesty. Damon doesn't shy away from the missteps and the hard-earned lessons that shaped the success of his company. This isn't a story of a company that got it right from the start; it's a far more relatable and valuable narrative about a company that dared to believe it could be better and then did the hard work to make that belief a reality. A changemaker at heart!"

Deke Copenhaver
Former Mayor, Augusta, Georgia; bestselling author,
The Changemaker: The Art of Building Better Leaders

"It's rare that a business book provides unique insights, and at the same time, is compelling throughout and entertaining to read. *Believe in Better* hits all of these high marks and covers a broad spectrum of topics that founders and executives struggle with every day. Not only a must and informative read, but a pleasurable one."

David Turner
CEO, Velocity Now

"*Believe in Better* is a compelling and insightful exploration of the entrepreneurial journey, resonating deeply with the chal-lenges and triumphs I've witnessed in the HR industry. Stafford offers a masterful guide to evolving business principles in a rapidly changing corporate landscape. His story is a testament to the power of adaptability, continuous improvement, and the relentless pursuit of excellence. This book is an invaluable resource for any business leader striving to scale their company while maintaining a steadfast commitment to their core values."

Bill Lyons

Founder and Executive Chairman, Lyons HR; Bestselling Author, We Are HR

"Believe in Better by Damon Stafford is a masterclass in entrepreneurial resilience and innovation, embodying the GRITT principles of being Goal-Driven, Responsible, Involved, Team-oriented, and Tolerant of failure. Stafford's corporate journey resonates with the core of my own philosophy in Keeping Score with GRITT. This book is an essential read for anyone looking to navigate the complexities of business growth with tenacity and a steadfast commitment to evolving core values."

Shawn Burcham

Founder and CEO, PFSbrands; bestselling author of Keeping Score with GRITT

"Believe in Better is a testament to the power of resilience, adaptability, and the relentless pursuit of excellence. Damon Stafford's candid recount of his company's meteoric rise to an industry titan is not just inspiring—it's a blueprint for any entrepreneur who finds themselves navigating the treacherous waters of business growth and scaling. This guy is the epitome of a professional problem solver."

Marc LaFleur

Bestselling author, True Founder

BELIEVE IN BETTER

Believe in Better

in Better

Damon Stafford

Forbes | Books

Published by Forbes Books, Charleston, South Carolina.
An imprint of Advantage Media Group.

Forbes Books is a registered trademark, and the Forbes Books colophon is a trademark of Forbes Media, LLC.

Printed in the United States of America.

10 9 8 7 6 5 4 3 2 1

ISBN: 979-8-88750-146-8 (Hardcover)
ISBN: 979-8-88750-147-5 (eBook)

Library of Congress Control Number: 2024900711

Cover and layout design by Matthew Morse.

This custom publication is intended to provide accurate information and the opinions of the author in regard to the subject matter covered. It is sold with the understanding that the publisher, Forbes Books, is not engaged in rendering legal, financial, or professional services of any kind. If legal advice or other expert assistance is required, the reader is advised to seek the services of a competent professional.

Since 1917, Forbes has remained steadfast in its mission to serve as the defining voice of entrepreneurial capitalism. Forbes Books, launched in 2016 through a partnership with Advantage Media, furthers that aim by helping business and thought leaders bring their stories, passion, and knowledge to the forefront in custom books. Opinions expressed by Forbes Books authors are their own. To be considered for publication, please visit **books.Forbes.com**.

To Sugie, Sullivan, and Callahan

Contents

Introduction

Do not bother just to be better than your contemporaries or predecessors. Try to be better than yourself.

—WILLIAM FAULKNER

On the inaugural day of my newly launched InsurTech company, the air was filled with a mixture of excitement and uncertainty, with Pearl Jam's *Vs.* album at an unhealthy volume. To say I was elated would be an understatement. Leaving IBM behind, I was ready to revel in the newfound sense of entrepreneurship. My Blackberry buzzed with updates, indicating the twenty open orders that we'd begun with. A celebratory beer was on my horizon.

But just as I was preparing to toast to a new beginning, my phone rang with a notification that would forever change my perspective. It was the top executive from an insurance carrier, and she wasn't calling with congratulations. In a tone thick with frustration, she unleashed a tirade, questioning the integrity and viability of our business model. "This is the worst company I've ever seen. Who even owns this?" she snapped. Her biting words culminated with, "Your model is a disaster."

I was dumbstruck. But before I could delve into self-pity, I realized the situation provided clarity. A policyholder had been without air conditioning for ten days, and when our team arrived the very next day after we received the order, they were under the impression we were there to fix it immediately. The insurance carrier, our client, believed the same. Instead, our role was to inspect, diagnose, and report the facts. The chasm in communication was evident.

We absolutely delivered on what we said we were going to do. But if one customer had purchased our services thinking we provided a totally different value, what about our other customers? Could it be possible that they, too, bought our services thinking we would provide something completely different? What if this was going to be one of many unpleasant calls to come? It's one thing to have an unhappy customer; it's another when that unhappiness arises from the same issue repeatedly. We had a glaring problem, and patching it up wasn't the solution. Because Band-Aids aren't sustainable. The real task was to eliminate the root of our recurring injuries.

So after countless hours of brainstorming—not to mention the clock ticking away within the entrepreneurial pressure cooker of trying to get the business off the ground—we formulated a communication process. The challenge was monumental with my limited resources, but we wove it into our business model with the application of tech wherever possible in our processes. And it's a good thing we did. Fast-forward to our current clientele of tens of thousands of policyholders per month. Imagine the sheer volume of complaints had we not committed to improving our communications and our process.

That phone call, on the proverbial day one, was a brutal awakening. But it was also a blessing in disguise. Ultimately it was survival, no turning back. It underscored the ever-pressing need to not just be good, but to commit to be better.

Always.

Where did that commitment to be better get us? Over five hundred team members and a valuation of over half a billion dollars at the time of this writing. It's taken my team and I well over a decade to achieve this kind of overnight success. And we did it by believing we could be better.

There are endless books out there about businesses that had their core principles for success baked right into their corporate DNA from the beginning. This is NOT that book. *Believe in Better: The Evolution of Core Principles That Pioneered an Industry* is the business book for the rest of us. For those who figure things out as we go along, always working to make tomorrow better than yesterday.

I imagine you may have a few burning questions by this point, the least of which being, *what the hell is InsurTech?* When I started the company a dozen years ago, the definition of InsurTech was fresh to say the least; a term backpacked on the financial community's success of FinTech. First of all, rest assured this book is NOT about InsurTech. Those within this niche industry will find it interesting from a professional perspective to be sure. But knowledge about InsurTech is not a requisite quality to access the utility of this book.

For the insatiably curious, however, InsurTech is the unification of new technology (software and structured data) to the legacy insurance model. The application of technology empowers insurance carriers to influence real change across their business, allowing them to make better decisions, mitigate risk, take market share from competitors and better serve their policyholders (you and me). When insurance companies run more efficiently, then consumers of insurance (like you and me) can see the benefit of InsurTech via lower premiums paid.

The value delivered to insurance carriers (aka the customer, a rarely referenced word corporate America) when I started the company was focused on value created by digitization of paper processes, coincidently a war that other industries won in the previous decade, creating synchronous software interfaces to eliminate data entry from the field, nimble technology built on the cloud and not on your grandpa's servers (btw I made a killing selling maintenance contracts on these things back in the day at IBM), on getting expensive fingers off of keyboards by eliminating duplication of data, and by applying the technologies used by the rest of the business and consumer world—such as basic logistical routing technologies. To put it in perspective, at the point in time when I launched this company, Uber was still using Google for their ride logistics directions and routing. It was roughly 2011 when they changed their name from UberCab to Uber and hired their first computational neuroscientists who came on the scene like a "millennial firecracker" (quote from the movie *The Gentlemen*, in case you are wondering) to change the game as we know it.

Still confused? Imagine your air-conditioning system fails during a hot summer day, and a heating and air company you called comes out to fix your system and pump cool air into your home. The company sends a technician a day or two later and suggests that a recent lightning storm might be the culprit. Oh, and it's going to cost $12,000 to replace the air-conditioning system—soup to nuts. Every part, piece, and component.

In a world before my first company, most people's next step would be to file a claim with their insurance carrier or insurance agent. After routing the claim, the complexity kicks off internal processes at the insurance carrier, which takes days of fist pounding for everyone involved in order to reach a decision. Not to mention, it's very likely the insurance carrier might just pay you $10,000 or more, no questions asked. If this doesn't seem like a bad outcome, stay tuned for the punch line.

They wouldn't probe into whether the damage was due to a lightning strike or an elephant standing on it, what the actual repair costs were, or if the system could have been repaired instead of being replaced. Google *environmental impact of HVAC industry* or *refrigerant* for the absurd truth. This lack of detailed assessment or factual understanding of the right repair method and market costs translates into billions in unchecked expenditures for insurance carriers. And guess what that does to the industry? It spikes all of our monthly premium payments to insurance companies. We *all* end up paying for it.

Enter Alpine Intel (formerly CCG IQ). Recognizing this glaring gap, we position ourselves strategically as subject matter experts for insurance carriers. The insurance company still runs their same internal processes through the required steps for approval, but in one-tenth the time because they have all the facts to make a fair decision. The homeowner gets cool air faster with time and expense saved.

But crafting this business wasn't a walk in the park. The tech in InsurTech is our relentless focus on technology enablement and developer expertise who turn what previously took weeks into days, hours, and nanoseconds, automating every possible step in the process. The company kick-started the old-fashioned way, from bonus checks from my employer and cashing out 401(k) plans at the age of thirty-one. Its first digital presence, a website developed from a template written in German during nights and weekends. In an era when cloud technology was blossoming and an 800 number became affordable for the first time, I traded IT contacts for insurance leads, created targeted email templates, and began reaching out with a straightforward value proposition. "We have experts who will give you the truth you've always wanted and needed on A, B, and C," the pitch went. "We can provide a detailed, fair report for your claim decision within three business days." Before our company, it could take as long as fifteen days for a decision. The business model was lean, bootstrapped, and entirely hands-on—from scheduling to report writing.

This wasn't just about being a disruptor; it was about adding substantive, tangible value to our customers, one transaction at a time. And it caught on. What began as a small operation soon transformed into a real, thriving business, changing the game for insurance carriers and their policyholders alike.

In essence, Alpine Intel and our InsurTech model epitomize what W. Chan Kim and Renée Mauborgne describe in their bestselling book *Blue Ocean Strategy*. Instead of wrestling with competitors in the saturated market (the "red ocean"), we crafted an uncontested space, where the competition was irrelevant because we were solving a unique, widespread problem in a novel way.

While many companies may boast about their technological capabilities, Alpine Intel's core strength lies in its unwavering commitment to an unparalleled customer experience, with a focus on solving boring, age-old problems while delighting our customers with a fresh way of doing business. Then we apply our technology horsepower and it's game over. This is based on our core values:

- We do what we say we will do.
- We are easy to do business with.
- We innovate by simplifying the complex.
- We solve quantifiable problems.
- We give credit where due.
- We embrace change.

Believe in Better is my journey to discover these core values, based on the business principles detailed in the chapters ahead—evergreen principles like transparency, teamwork, and embracing change. Whether you are a C-suite exec or a senior leader embedded deep in the unique InsurTech space, or maybe you are a hungry entrepreneur who is simply looking for tried-and-true guidance on evolving your own core business principles, this book is a journey that is certain to entertain, enlighten, and inspire.

Notice I didn't write a book called *Believe in Best* or *Believe in Perfection*. Run as far and as fast as you can away from anyone trying to sell a book like that, because they are likely invoking some kind of revisionist history bullshit. Because perfection is an intangible ideal. And the concept of *best* is temporary at, well, best. No matter what industry you are in, you will never be the best for long. Look at professional football, for instance. Why do you think every single team in the league grinds it out season after season? Because you only get to be the Superbowl champ for a year. Then either you defend it or someone else takes your place. The same with every Fortune 500 company that has ever existed. Those firms are always being ranked, evaluated, and measured. There's always going to be competition. And the higher you climb, the bigger the bull's-eye on your metaphoric back becomes.

To succeed in business, in anything really, you need to become obsessed with being *better*. How can I be a better leader? How can we offer better customer service? How can we sell better? How can we work better as a team? How can we have better transparency as a company? How can we embrace change better?

If you really want to be the best, you need to focus on being better. In all departments. At all times. That's where this book comes in.

Written by a guy that held sales call contests at the age of 23 that ended with the loser dancing in the busy parking lot in front of an eight-story office building, forcing the loser to do a solo dance (unaccompanied by music) for exactly three minutes while the pack of other twenty-something wanna-be professionals huddled and watched from the comfort of their window.

A guy who found out 20 years later that the garden I was forced to care for as a kid was a different kind of cabbage. Which explains all those helicopters.

A guy just like you, with epic stories from college that will never be told—except the few in this book.

A guy who is a devoted husband and father, running an organization of 500 people and nearing a billion in valuation, based on real profit and a real company—one that I started a dozen years ago.

So why did I write this book? For that feeling of release that comes when creating something. For that feeling of excitement when putting pen to paper, so maybe someone who reads it will want to be a part of our team and help us take our organization to a level beyond our wildest dreams. To illustrate to our customers how hard our employees work for them and have the best interests of their policyholders in mind. To call out all of the jackasses I've been around in the business world over the years. To maybe meet some new people. Definitely not to make coin on writing a book—seems as if that's an impossible feat.

To this end, I've identified ten key areas within the realm of business that will drive unprecedented success and growth when you simply focus on being *better*.

These ten areas make up the chapters of this book, chock-full of real-life anecdotes, gems of wisdom, and practical tactics for making your business better.

And each chapter wraps with a short, cautionary fairy tale related to the principle discussed, like the one below.

Once upon a time, in the high-rising kingdom of Corporatopia, there was a CEO named Egoton who believed he was the best. He strutted around with his American Express Black Card, throwing it like a ninja star at anyone who dared meet his eye. His company was at the top of the charts, and Egoton felt he had reached the pinnacle of success.

But in the neighboring district of Innovasia, a young entrepreneur named Ambitia was not content with just being the best. She aimed to be better. While Egoton was busy basking in the temporary sunlight of his accomplishments, Ambitia was innovating, learning, and redefining her own success.

One day, as the story goes, Egoton's AmEx Black Card lost its luster. His employees started leaving in droves for Ambitia's company. Egoton's company crumbled, outdated and outmaneuvered. He tried to recover, enrolling in endless masterclasses and taking up hot yoga. He read every business book out there (except this one).

But it was too fucking late. Ambitia's business bloomed, transforming the market in ways previously unimaginable. Egoton's business model and skill sets were now obsolete. He was relegated to living off Arby's Horsey Sauce, stealing packets and selling them outside Ambitia's new downtown headquarters.

The lesson? Being the best is fleeting, but striving to be better is forever. So, before you decide to rest on your laurels like Egoton, ask yourself: Do I want to be just the best, or do I want to be better?

Now, let's turn the page and see how you can do just that.

BELIEVE IN BETTER / THE EVOLUTION OF CORE PRINCIPLES
THAT PIONEERED AN INDUSTRY // **AUTHENTICITY MAKES
YOU BETTER** // BELIEVE IN BETTER / THE EVOLUTION
OF CORE PRINCIPLES THAT PIONEERED AN INDUSTRY //
HUSTLING MAKES YOU BETTER // BELIEVE IN BETTER /
THE EVOLUTION OF CORE PRINCIPLES THAT PIONEERED AN
INDUSTRY // BELIEVE IN BETTER / THE EVOLUTION OF CORE
PRINCIPLES THAT PIONEERED AN INDUSTRY // SELLING
MAKES YOU BETTER // BELIEVE IN BETTER / THE EVOLUTION
OF CORE PRINCIPLES THAT PIONEERED AN INDUSTRY //
BELIEVE IN BETTER / THE EVOLUTION OF CORE PRINCIPLES
THAT PIONEERED AN INDUSTRY // BELIEVE IN BETTER /
THE EVOLUTION OF CORE PRINCIPLES THAT PIONEERED AN
INDUSTRY // BELIEVE IN BETTER / THE EVOLUTION OF CORE
PRINCIPLES THAT PIONEERED AN INDUSTRY // UNDERSTANDING
PERSPECTIVE MAKES YOU BETTER //BELIEVE IN BETTER /
THE EVOLUTION OF CORE PRINCIPLES THAT PIONEERED AN
INDUSTRY // BELIEVE IN BETTER / THE EVOLUTION OF CORE
PRINCIPLES THAT PIONEERED AN INDUSTRY // TEAMWORK
MAKES YOU BETTER // BELIEVE IN BETTER / THE EVOLUTION
OF CORE PRINCIPLES THAT PIONEERED AN INDUSTRY //
TAKING ACTION MAKES YOU BETTER // BELIEVE IN BETTER
/ THE EVOLUTION OF CORE PRINCIPLES THAT PIONEERED A
INDUSTRY // TRANSPARENCY MAKES YOU BETTER // BELIEV
IN BETTER / THE EVOLUTION OF CORE PRINCIPLES THAT
PIONEERED AN INDUSTRY // DRIVING PROFITABILITY MAKE
YOU BETTER // THE EVOLUTION OF CORE PRINCIPLES THA
PIONEERED AN INDUSTRY // PROCESS MAKES YOU BETTER /
BELIEVE IN BETTER / THE EVOLUTION OF CORE PRINCIPLE
THAT PIONEERED AN INDUSTRY // CHANGE MAKES YOU BETTE
// BELIEVE IN BETTER / THE EVOLUTION OF CORE PRINCIPL

Authenticity Makes You Better

Be yourself, everyone else is taken.

—OSCAR WILDE

I was at a corporate event in New York recently where there happened to be an after-hours poker game for some of the attendees. I enjoy a friendly game of poker just as much as the next guy, and I knew these people fairly well. One was a Harvard grad, another studied at Yale, an MIT alum, Princeton—you get the picture. I went to a good college, nothing in the Ivy League category. And I've never put much stock into judging a person by the price of tuition for the school they attended. But I also know when to be realistic.

We're talking about people who likely took electives on game theory and laws of probability *and* majored in computer science or artificial intelligence. Their mental processing power subconsciously runs through mathematical equations when simply making a decision on what flavor of Doritos to buy. So what did I say when they invited me to join them?

"Fuck, no. I'm going to sip tequila and go see what this fresh-rolled cigar bar is all about."

Everybody laughed. And they still laugh and talk about that maneuver to this day. Granted, being a Yale graduate does not guarantee that a person will be good at poker. Many other factors, such as experience, skill, and personal style, can also play a role in determining success at the poker table. But I didn't want to take that chance. Sure, I could have faked it and lost my shirt. But by being authentic, I won even more than whatever the pot they were playing for was worth. I earned their respect.

That was just me being myself, because honestly I don't know how to be anybody else. In fact, there isn't a "business" Damon and a "personal" Damon. Love me or hate me, I'm the same person at the board table as at the dinner table. I'd argue that's been a key to making me better—authenticity.

The Damon writing this book is a bit professional and a bit personal, a guy who has evolved over time with no plans on stopping. I remember early on in my career saying some really embarrassing things—using terminology out of context and casually dropping words with nine syllables—because that's what I thought I needed to say to be accepted in the business world. But as I started to bring the real Damon in, my thoughts became clearer and my communication with others better.

And part of communication getting better is learning how to listen authentically.

Listen Authentically

Within our leadership team, everyone knows I'm authentic with them. They know the real me, which means they can smell bullshit a mile away. They might not like what I have to say all the time, but they know I will always listen to them.

Leaders can never underestimate the power of authentic listening, not just sitting there nodding like a bobblehead on a hot dashboard. All too often we sit in meetings with empty suits who aren't really listening—they are waiting for their turn so they can say whatever it is they want to say. How is that communication? I'm not saying it doesn't happen where I'm sitting there waiting to inject a particularly powerful point into the conversation. But I try to keep myself in check as much as possible because I know—we all know— the feeling of talking with someone whose eyes have that checked-out, glazed look. Or even better, those people who are chomping at the bit, revving their engine to get their next comment out.

> **Leaders can never underestimate the power of authentic listening.**

I've actually evolved to the point of taking it a step further. If I find that I myself have checked out of a conversation for whatever reason, I hold myself accountable right to the person speaking. In fact, I often say the following for effect: "I didn't hear one single word that came out of your mouth for the last sixty seconds. Sorry!"

It's definitely not a comfortable situation, but I guarantee the person will feel respected—and, more importantly, *heard*—if you demonstrate the courage to listen authentically. And I've found that somehow, someway, that kind of authenticity boomerangs back in your favor. After all, just pretending like you heard someone is nothing but a cover-up for your gap in audible skills. It's dysfunctional and unproductive. Is a conversation really worth having if you are not in sync throughout it? What's wrong with a pause and reset to ensure the rest of the meeting isn't a complete waste of time?

Being authentic, however, doesn't mean you need to throw all your shortcomings out on the table for the world to gawk at. Some things are definitely better left unseen.

Don't Show All Your Cards

Steve Mauldin, a great buddy of mine, once told me, "You can be genuine and authentic, yet not show all your cards." That couldn't be truer, especially in really awkward or high-risk situations. That doesn't mean you have permission to *not* be authentic. You still need to be yourself. But you don't have to tell the other person *everything*. Incidentally, no one in the world is better at this skillful balancing act than my wife.

When I was first getting our InsurTech business off the ground, a major insurance carrier heard about our services and wanted to learn more. As expected, they needed to size us up and vet us on our national presence, so they checked out our website, our marketing materials, which were all top notch. Then they asked to come for a site visit at our office in Charlotte, North Carolina. The thing was, our office had a whopping three rooms and looked like, well, just picture a cross between a massage studio and an old-school lawyer's office with low ceilings and fizzling, fluorescent lighting.

"Sure, we'd be happy to host you," I told the insurance carrier executive. We had all the capabilities to service his company, but we were a small team. Our white tablecloth entertaining and corporate procurement onboarding processes weren't very sophisticated. I wore many hats in those days. But I wasn't about to put up a facade that we were something we weren't. I also didn't necessarily intend to reveal all our cards either, just give them what they needed to make a decision and buy our services at a national scale. So this big national player showed up, and I sat with him for hours in my little office—a space so small that the thirty-two-inch flat screen I was projecting to was nearly resting on my left shoulder during the entire presentation. But I made it work, and I answered as many questions as I could—redirecting those I couldn't for follow-up.

> **Being genuine with who you are creates instant confidence, and with confidence you can influence.**

I'm happy to say that authenticity won the day. We ended up landing the account, and it was game on from there. But I learned a valuable lesson: being genuine with who you are creates instant confidence, and with confidence you can influence—or, in this case, close a deal that changes your life forever.

But only if you live really truly, *live* authentically. Not sometimes. Not most of the time. *All the time.*

Authenticity Is a Lifestyle

Early in my career, I sold recruitment services to supply medical professionals to hospitals—people who could operate, maintain, and perform diagnostic procedures with magnetic resonance imaging (MRI) and computed tomography (CT) scan machines, for example. The thing was, I had nothing tangible to sell the prospect sitting across from me. I was essentially selling myself first to build rapport and trust and then my company's services. That's when I realized authenticity in business is everything. People can sniff out an inauthentic salesperson a mile away. That's probably why sales has such a bad reputation—inauthentic salespeople saying and doing anything just trying to close business. There's a lot more on how selling makes you better in chapter three, but authenticity is intimately woven into the fabric of sales. Because if you aren't real with customers, you will never earn their trust, no matter how great your product or service is.

Mark Twain said, "If you tell the truth, you don't have to remember anything." The same principle applies to being authentic. If you live an authentic lifestyle, you never have to worry about how you are being perceived or if you are communicating clearly.

I tell our sales teams all the time that if you are selling a service, taking business from competitors is as easy as confidently communicating that our people are the best, better than the competitor. Half the battle is whether or not that carrier believes what we are saying. It doesn't mean we're going to win their business, but if we are authentic, at least we give ourselves a fighting chance. And if we win the business, authenticity is what maintains that relationship. You need to deliver what you promised to deliver.

If you think you're going to fake it, I promise you that somebody's going to sniff you out sooner or later and call bullshit.

And if things don't go perfectly, be open with the client. Because nothing ever goes as planned in business, especially when technology is involved. And trust me, the person (emphasis here on the word *person*) whom you are talking with has certainly made mistakes in life and—unless they are a complete psychopath—can empathize with someone who is admitting they made a mistake *and* have a plan for it to not happen again. The only thing you do have control over is your genuine concern and willingness to make things right when things go sideways.

Like the time one of our former medical technicians with a clean background check was found passed out in the parking lot of a hospital on a day he wasn't even scheduled to work. The tech was arrested, but to make things right, I called the director of radiology and genuinely explained the situation, apologizing profusely. An apology that came with commitment to anonymously fund the employee holiday party. Would the director have found out about my nuclear medicine tech who was handcuffed in the visitor parking lot of the hospital and locked up for half a doobie in their ashtray, not for driving under the influence (DUI)? Probably, but maybe not. Needless to say, authenticity won the day, and the next week I picked up an order for three more positions to fill at the hospital because of the trust I built. Trust built on a very bad situation.

If you think you're going to fake it, I promise you that somebody's going to sniff you out sooner or later and call bullshit. If you are speaking with whoever is "in power," someone who has a vested interest or responsibility in making the right decision, and their livelihood is dependent on the right decision, you might hear what you want to hear—that you are "on fire" selling—but you probably aren't talking to the right person. There are a lot of smart people in the world, people like private equity and venture capitalists, who make a lot of money by gauging and sniffing out who's authentic and who's not. At the end of the day, they are just placing bets on people. Do they believe the person making the pitch? Do they believe the passion? If you've ever watched *Shark Tank*, you know the sharks are really investing in people, not in a product or a service.

It's easy to be authentic with things you are very knowledgeable or passionate about. Not so much when you aren't. That's when you need to hack your authenticity.

Hacking Your Authenticity

We've all been there—needing to get up in front of a bunch of people and make a presentation when we have zero motivation. Maybe it's due to so many conflicting priorities. Or maybe it's because we need to deliver a message we're not totally aligned with. Whatever the case, our hearts are just not in it. The Passion Police unknowingly pulled you over on the way to work, confiscated all the passion that brought you to that moment, and now you end up just mailing it in, saying what you think everyone wants to hear just to get it over with. I refer to this as "reading the news." If you are just going to read the news, then send a freaking email. Don't waste your time or theirs.

This is when you need to hack your authenticity with some Jedi mind tricks. There's a cognitive specialist named Beatrice Moise, MS, BCCS, from North Carolina who wrote a book called *Our Neurodivergent Journey*. In this book, she talks about the importance of taking a few minutes before undertaking a task you don't want to do to psych yourself up with self-talk by pausing and getting in the right headspace to genuinely convince *yourself* that this meeting, this task, is important. And don't leave the moment until you have truly convinced yourself. Otherwise, no one else will believe you.

When I had a full day of two-hour interviews to fill an open position on my executive leadership team, I can authentically say I was dreading it. But I took some time beforehand to tell myself how important the meeting would be for the business, for my team, for my family! How much time would be wasted if we *didn't* make the right hire! How motivating would it be for the rest of the team if I indeed found an ace!

It might sound crazy, but I got myself all pumped up—dare I say *excited*—for the meeting after hacking my authenticity. Not in the Dwight from *The Office* sort of way—the headbanging-to-Mötley Crüe-in-your-car-before-a-sales-call routine—but in a genuine, thoughtful way to find the moment, and therefore the pressure to get your mind sharp to perform, because it's *that* important. Because if you don't have *your own* buy-in on something, it will show through. There's no shame in being authentic with yourself about where your motivations lie.

We have so many distractions in life. And as your business grows, you're only going to get more distracted. You're always going to have certain passions you could talk about at the drop of a hat, but never underestimate the power of hacking your authenticity when needed. It shows you value authenticity above all else.

And if you value your own authenticity, you sure as hell can demand it from others.

Demand Authenticity

I've always admired the person who flat out says they didn't finish college instead of sugar-coating their education during an interview. As previously stated, I'm not one to judge someone on their academic accomplishments or professional shortcomings. I care more about ability and authenticity, which create that spark of charisma. In fact, people who try their best to be authentic demand it from other people. I know I do of my team.

We recently went through an exercise of reviewing our operating principles. One of the principles we adopted is: We trust that all our team members have positive intentions and give one another permission to be challenged. This safe space to "say it here and now" allows us to seek to understand with candor and gives us clarity in decision-making. With these principles in place, we have genuine alignment to execute our plans without hindsight. Basically, if you have an opinion, voice it. There's not going to be a meeting after the meeting. There's not going to be a hallway conversation to make a different decision. This isn't unique to our company. Many companies employ this principle, but we live and die by it. It generates a lot of energy that creates healthy tension and stress.

People who say "I took the high road" or "I was the bigger person" typically don't have the strength to confront others or have a healthy debate. Especially in the southern US, we have what we affectionately call "bless your hearts" everywhere. The great news though is that if you create this environment—and you live by it—you will instantly rise to the top and demand authority from others. As an executive or employee of my company, everyone knows they have an obligation to be authentic in front of their colleagues. Engaging in tough conversations is part of the job. In fact, if you are on my leadership team or a manager of any part of the organization, then it's a responsibility. Because from my point of view, *that's what the money is for!*

To get to this position as a company, we needed to define that everybody on the team has positive intentions. No one is going to delight in shooting down another's ideas. And if you assume that everyone has positive intentions, then you have to be open to and comfortable with conflict, with people probing and pressing and asking questions. You can't take it personally. Because I've known companies that have meetings, then meetings after meetings, and then secret meetings after meetings, which all result in a lack of efficiency, poor communication, and disharmony. Paving the way for less than optimal outcomes.

Suddenly meetings become a waste of time, so they discontinue them. No successful company in their right mind *can* NOT have meetings. Therefore, meetings need to be productive. And productive meetings demand authenticity, which creates a positive friction that forces forward movement. It's my job as the leader of the organization to make sure anyone who does not have positive intentions or best intentions for the team, the company, our employees, and our shareholders are walked out of the door.

But authenticity will do a lot more for your business than simply improving the productivity of meetings. It will make your business better.

A Fairy Tale about Authenticity

Once upon a time, there was a small honeycomb business, Three Bears Inc., which prided itself in providing high-quality honey and exceptional customer service to bear families and their cubs deep in the forest. The owners of the business believed that their furry customers deserved only the best, and they were determined to deliver just that.

> **Productive meetings demand authenticity, which creates a positive friction that forces forward movement.**

However, as the business grew, the owners realized that their focus on authenticity was beginning to slip. They were making decisions based on what they thought would bring in the most profit rather than what was truly in the best interest of their customers. They noticed that their customer satisfaction ratings were starting to decline, and they were losing the trust and loyalty of their customers.

The owners of the business decided that they needed to refocus on authenticity and make it the cornerstone of their operations. They took a step back and re-evaluated their mission and values and made a commitment to always put their customers first. They also made sure that their employees were aligned with their values and understood the importance of providing genuine, personalized service to each and every honeycomb client.

With their renewed focus on authenticity, the business was ready to thrive again. The Three Bears Inc. management team was rejuvenated and full of energy. But it was too fucking late.

Competitors passed them by, the honeycomb customers moved on, the market shifted, new investors entered the market, and employees got burned out. For the leadership of Three Bears Inc., it was far worse than getting caught with their collective pants down. They were Winnie-the-Poohed—shocked and dismayed and relegated to wearing nothing but questionably short T-shirts and no pants.

One of their competitors, Goldilocks Ltd., understood the need for authenticity all along. With her focus on authenticity, her business began to thrive where Three Bears had failed. Customer satisfaction rates were at an all-time high, and the business started attracting a new generation of loyal customers who appreciated the genuine, high-quality products and services that Goldilocks Ltd. provided.

Goldi and her husband were overjoyed to see their business succeed and proud to have built a reputation as one of the most authentic businesses in the industry. They continued to strive for excellence and to always put their customers first, and their business continued to flourish for many years to come.

The leadership of Three Bears, however, was forced to bumble around a cardboard cut-out of the Hundred Acre Wood in a flea market parking lot, handing out red balloons and taking pictures with whiny kids.

Don't you love happy endings? Authenticity in business impacts a company's reputation, customer satisfaction, and overall success. By always putting customers first and staying true to your values, your business will build a loyal following and establish itself as a leader in your industry.

Reflections for Believing in Better

Authenticity in business is important because it helps to build trust and credibility, differentiate from competitors, improve reputation, attract top talent, and foster employee engagement. Here are a few reflection points to make the road to believing in better, well, better.

- **Building Trust:** Authenticity builds trust with customers and stakeholders, creating a stronger relationship based on transparency and honesty.
- **Enhancing Reputation:** Authentic businesses have a more positive reputation, as they are perceived as being genuine and trustworthy.
- **Differentiation:** Authenticity helps businesses to differentiate themselves from competitors, as customers are drawn to unique, genuine experiences.
- **Increased Loyalty:** Authentic businesses often have a higher level of customer loyalty, as customers feel a personal connection to the company and its values.
- **Attracting Talent:** Authentic companies often have a strong employer brand, attracting top talent who are drawn to their values and culture.
- **Boosting Employee Engagement:** Employees are more likely to be engaged and motivated in a work environment that values authenticity and aligns with their own personal values.

BELIEVE IN BETTER / THE EVOLUTION OF CORE PRINCIPLE
THAT PIONEERED AN INDUSTRY // AUTHENTICITY MAKE
YOU BETTER // BELIEVE IN BETTER / THE EVOLUTIO
OF CORE PRINCIPLES THAT PIONEERED AN INDUSTRY /
HUSTLING MAKES YOU BETTER // BELIEVE IN BETTER
THE EVOLUTION OF CORE PRINCIPLES THAT PIONEERED A
INDUSTRY // BELIEVE IN BETTER / THE EVOLUTION OF COR
PRINCIPLES THAT PIONEERED AN INDUSTRY // SELLIN
MAKES YOU BETTER // BELIEVE IN BETTER / THE EVOLUTIO
OF CORE PRINCIPLES THAT PIONEERED AN INDUSTRY /
BELIEVE IN BETTER / THE EVOLUTION OF CORE PRINCIPLE
THAT PIONEERED AN INDUSTRY // BELIEVE IN BETTER
THE EVOLUTION OF CORE PRINCIPLES THAT PIONEERED A
INDUSTRY // BELIEVE IN BETTER / THE EVOLUTION OF COR
PRINCIPLES THAT PIONEERED AN INDUSTRY // UNDERSTANDIN
PERSPECTIVE MAKES YOU BETTER //BELIEVE IN BETTER
THE EVOLUTION OF CORE PRINCIPLES THAT PIONEERED A
INDUSTRY // BELIEVE IN BETTER / THE EVOLUTION OF COR
PRINCIPLES THAT PIONEERED AN INDUSTRY // TEAMWOR
MAKES YOU BETTER // BELIEVE IN BETTER / THE EVOLUTIO
OF CORE PRINCIPLES THAT PIONEERED AN INDUSTRY /
TAKING ACTION MAKES YOU BETTER // BELIEVE IN BETTE
/ THE EVOLUTION OF CORE PRINCIPLES THAT PIONEERED A
INDUSTRY // TRANSPARENCY MAKES YOU BETTER // BELIEV
IN BETTER / THE EVOLUTION OF CORE PRINCIPLES THA
PIONEERED AN INDUSTRY // DRIVING PROFITABILITY MAKE
YOU BETTER // THE EVOLUTION OF CORE PRINCIPLES THA
PIONEERED AN INDUSTRY // PROCESS MAKES YOU BETTER /
BELIEVE IN BETTER / THE EVOLUTION OF CORE PRINCIPLE
THAT PIONEERED AN INDUSTRY // CHANGE MAKES YOU BETTE
// BELIEVE IN BETTER / THE EVOLUTION OF CORE PRINCIPL

Hustling Makes You Better

Things may come to those who wait …
but only the things left by those who hustle.

—ABRAHAM LINCOLN

Not long ago, I needed to fly to Vegas to open our new office and lab facility, cut the ribbon, and spend a little time with our team. Knowing it was a four-and-a-half-hour flight, I made sure I was sitting beside my CFO so we could knock some work out while in the air. After we landed, we were picked up by the people who run the lab and brought through on a tour. When the tour was over, we could have just returned to the hotel and crashed—after all, it had been a long day of traveling and meetings, right? But no, we stayed another two and a half hours and talked about our tactical plan for growth with the team and incentive plans to hit our revenue projections.

At that point, the rest of the free world would go off and enjoy a night on the town in Vegas. Not me. While walking to the hotel front desk to grab my bags and get a room key, I checked in on my phone for my six o'clock flight in the morning, which incidentally was eleven hours away because I wanted to make sure I was back with my family for the weekend. That was the first breath I had taken so far in Vegas. And I still hadn't stepped foot in my hotel room, consisting of circa 1960 Rat-Pack-at-the-Sands décor.

The rest of the night consisted of making some memories and playing cards with my team in a forced but genuine fire-drill celebration for working so hard to hit the new facility move-in date. At one point, I left the group to meet up with one of our partners' brother and sister-in-law who happened to live there. Because he had just started with the company, I wanted him and his family to feel appreciated and respected, like part of our corporate family.

Afterward, I went back downstairs to the card game to get a few more memories in with the team and then finally headed off to bed. I was absolutely crushed by that point. Four and a half hours later, the alarm went off. I dragged myself out of bed, got cleaned up, and groggily stumbled to the lobby so I could make my flight home.

Being engaged and making yourself accessible are critical for the growth and success of your company.

Sure, I could have stayed in Vegas for the week. I could have taken a later flight. I could have told my team I was exhausted and gracefully bowed out of dinner and card games. But as any good business leader knows, being engaged and making yourself accessible are critical for the growth and success of your company. And as any good parent and spouse knows, being engaged and making yourself accessible are critical for the growth and success of your family. Where the two converge can be problematic, unless you adopt a mentality of hustling.

The term *hustling* means different things to different people. To swindle, to hurry, to sell. To be clear, the definition of *hustle* that I'm referring to is akin to *industrious*—diligent and hardworking. Where you make the most of every moment personally and professionally. Where you create value in every action. Because hustling in the way I just described will make you better. But it's not a single event or a season. Hustling is about consistency and dedication. Hustling is not just about realizing, but accepting and embracing that time is your most precious resource.

It's in those moments when you force yourself to wake up at some ungodly hour just so you can drive your child to school. Not for the sake of getting them to school on time like some Uber driver but for the small window of connection you can have talking with them. They see you are present, that you care. To deliver even one small puzzle piece in their world of understanding. Maybe what it means truly to be kind, the difference between good or bad—or to know who artist Banksy is. To tell them before someone messes up the chance for you to explain the blurred lines that sometimes occur between right and wrong.

Because at the end of the day, hustling is more than an action.

Hustling Is a Lifestyle

I don't need to rewind very far to see that hustling has always been a part of who I am. After high school, I decided to disregard my stepfather's advice to skip a college education, skip trade school, and just learn a trade as an apprentice or journeyman. Instead, I opted for college, finding an in-state school that allowed me to join the

Crushing Student Loan Debt-Spiral for Eternity Club while also remaining as far from home as possible. Ultimately, I made the best decision I could have ever made at the time, eventually landing on East Carolina University.

The thing was, I didn't know a single person who went to school there. Complete blind faith. So it wasn't like I could lean on anyone or leverage connections to make things easier. I worked throughout my time there, including all holiday breaks. The word *worked* doesn't actually do it justice. I bussed tables and valeted cars at a local country club at night and worked days doing cable construction on the side of highways. Not to mention I grabbed any and all side work I possibly could, including heading home during the holidays to spray chemicals on Christmas trees at tree farms (chemicals that totally didn't affect my height or growth trajectory). My sophomore year I joined a fraternity and took the only jobs that didn't require you to pay dues, Treasurer and Social Chair. At one point I was actually doing both jobs, which may or may not have been a conflict of interest.

In addition to my courses, I was constantly putting on events to raise money for my fraternity and hiring bands for parties. I would find and book the bands, obtain the city noise ordinance, make sure the spiked punch was made according to our recipe (in a trash can), and even took money at the door. Afterward, it wasn't uncommon for me to flip the light switch on in my room at my fraternity—sending cockroaches scattering across the ceiling—so I could count the $10K in cash collected from the band party, all laid out across my bedspread. On top of it, I ran for Student Body vice president and traveled around in a van playing Club Ultimate Frisbee.

Call it hustling, but I wanted to experience it all, which I'd say is the case for most young men and women going to college. But I was the guy who managed to rip myself from my bed on four hours of sleep Friday morning to make sure I was in class by eight o'clock in the morning. I not only wanted it all, but I didn't want to fail at any of it as well. Or let anyone down.

On Friday nights, I would be right there with the last group of people still standing, into the wee hours of the morning. And then while everyone else was sleeping in and hungover, I'd head over to the football stadium to make sure the tailgate was set up for the fraternity. After a while, everyone would show up and start gameday festivities. Later, we'd all go to the game together. But as soon as halftime came, I'd make an Irish exit back to my room. Until my next obligation.

> **Hustling as a lifestyle doesn't guarantee success in business, but it does set the stage for it.**

Hustling as a lifestyle doesn't guarantee success in business, but it does set the stage for it. And by the way, I'm not the only one who operates at this intensity. Not by a long shot. We all know 'em, right? Maybe you are this exact person, with hustle on your breath and grit jammed between your teeth. When you think about it, this trait seems to be present in all those who are successful. Do they *need* to put themselves through this pain? Who knows! Maybe. Probably. Maybe smart entrepreneurs sleep twelve hours a day and hit their emails instead of trying to make their team feel connected and influencing through forming bonds, even when exhausted. Probably not though.

What does the research say? According to a survey by *Inc.* magazine, most successful entrepreneurs said that working hard was the most important factor in their success. Entrepreneurs who hustle often outperform their peers for a variety of reasons:

Increased Productivity: A study[1] published in the *Journal of Applied Psychology* found that employees who worked longer hours were more productive than those who worked shorter hours. This suggests that entrepreneurs who work harder and put in more time may be able to achieve more in their businesses.

More Opportunities: In a study[2] published in the *Journal of Business Venturing*, researchers found that entrepreneurs who were more proactive in seeking out opportunities tended to have more successful businesses. Hustling and putting in more effort can help entrepreneurs to identify and pursue more opportunities.

Improved Resilience: A study[3] published in the *Journal of Small Business Management* found that entrepreneurs who had a strong sense of resilience were more likely to succeed. Hustling and putting in more effort can help entrepreneurs to develop this sense of resilience.

Stronger Work Ethic: In a survey[4] of entrepreneurs conducted by *Inc.* magazine, the majority of respondents cited "working hard" as the most important factor in their success. This suggests that entrepreneurs who hustle tend to have a stronger work ethic than their peers.

1   Stacey R. Kessler and Nancy P. Rothbard, "Wharton Work/Life Integration Project: A Cross-Generational Study," *Journal of Applied Psychology* 100, no. 3 (2015): 776–808, doi: 10.1037/a0038852.

2   Susan A. Hill and Julian Birkinshaw, "Ambidexterity and Survival in Corporate Venture Units," *Journal of Business Venturing* 25, no. 5 (2010): 461–72, doi: 10.1016/j.jbusvent.2008.10.001.

3   Gaylen N. Chandler and Erik Jansen, "The Founder's Self-Assessed Competence and Venture Performance," *Journal of Small Business Management* 30, no. 3 (1992): 22–31, doi: 10.1111/j.1540-627x.1992.tb00534.x.

4   *Inc.*, "The State of Small Business: A Report from the Front Lines," 2014, accessed March 26, 2023, https://www.inc.com/special-reports/soty-state-of-small-business.html.

Improved Skill Set: A study[5] published in the *Journal of Business Venturing* found that entrepreneurs who had more experience in areas such as sales and marketing tended to have more successful businesses. Hustling and putting in more effort can help entrepreneurs to develop these skills.

Of course, there are many other factors that contribute to the success of entrepreneurs. But hustling is at the heart of it. There is a calling deep inside when hustling is a lifestyle. Almost a challenge. To get up early enough to take your children to school. To be the first in the office even when it hurts. To make the client lunch and five back-to-back Zoom calls afterward. And then get in my car and jam phone calls the entire way home, followed by sitting in my driveway with the car running to finish calls, only to hang up the call to hear three seconds of the song I've been listening to the entire week and haven't finished because I've been talking every moment possible. And then dinner with the family. Then follow through with the obligation you made to your client tonight, earlier than committed, even if you know you could get away with doing it first thing in the morning.

The thing is, there are only so many hours in a day. That means a key principle of hustling is understanding the economy of time, while balancing priorities of family and work.

Making Every Minute Count

In the days before you could go anywhere with a click, I did sales for a start-up medical company the hard way—literally door-to-door cold calls with hundreds of doctors. While the rest of the sales world would

---

5   Johan Wiklund and Dean Shepherd, "Portfolio Entrepreneurship: Habitual and
     Novice Founders, New Entry, and Mode of Organizing," *Journal of Business
     Venturing* 23, no. 4 (2008): 618–37, doi: 10.1016/j.jbusvent.2007.05.004.

wait until they got into the office each morning to decide what territory they were going to canvass and which doctors' offices they planned on targeting, I always *ended* each day with that sort of research while getting all my materials together. This meant driving back to the office when everyone was gone, getting MapQuest pulled up, and printing directions, which meant I was ready to dive right into sales calls without any delay bright and early every morning, which meant I could squeeze more calls into the average day than my peers. Simple strategy, eh? Sometimes the really hard work is in keeping it simple and executing on the fundamentals.

If reacting is part of your strategy because you never carve out time to think, you are wasting more than you are gaining, especially time.

On my way to my first sales call, I knew I had forty-seven minutes of drive time to just think, which is an overlooked and underappreciated function of business. Taking time to plan out my pitch or follow-up attempt to close a deal. Even taking the time to figure out how to pronounce the prospect's last name. All too often I've seen entrepreneurs run headlong from one task to another without taking the necessary time to think through any sort of comprehensive strategy. Then they react in the moment. I'm living proof, as even I still struggle with this. Don't get me wrong, the ability to react and adapt in the moment is a super valuable skill set. In fact, being "good in the pocket" ala Peyton Manning is kind of my superpower. But if reacting is part of your strategy because you never carve out time to think, you are wasting more than you are gaining, especially time.

Eventually I'd reach my target—the tallest medical building I could find—and I'd take the elevator to the top floor. Then I'd hit every single doctor's office and try to work my way into a meeting, finding an angle to establish credibility with people I'd never met, in a town I'd never been to in most cases. With a consultive sell in my back pocket paired with a compelling answer or follow-up meeting for every objection an MD could have. I just needed to get in the room! At least that's how it went in my mind, and I knew my trade better than they did. I'd usually end up saying just enough to get past the gatekeeper, just enough to get to the hallway to wait for the doctor. They wouldn't have time, and then I'd provide some proof points of what I was selling just to develop some momentum in the sales cycle. Sometimes they would be interested. Sometimes they wouldn't. Then I'd jog down a flight of stairs and do it again. Mind you, some of these were twenty-story buildings. Floor by floor, I got to know the cleaning crew on a first-name basis. But hustling is about economy of time, and the closer the proximity of targets I could find, the more efficient I was, and, in turn, successful.

It goes without saying that managing time effectively is crucial for the success of any business. With so many tasks and responsibilities to handle, it can be easy for business owners and employees to feel overwhelmed and fall behind schedule. But by understanding the economy of time in the context of hustling, individuals and teams can stay focused, meet deadlines, and achieve goals.

The ability to react and adapt in the moment is a super valuable skill set. But if reacting is part of your strategy because you never carve out time to think, you are wasting more than you are gaining, especially time.

Effective time management also helps to reduce stress and prevent burnout. When teams manage their time effectively, they are less likely to feel overwhelmed or overworked. This can improve morale, boost job satisfaction, and reduce turnover rates. Not to mention, making every second count helps to ensure that important tasks and deadlines are not overlooked or forgotten.

But how do you know if you are making every second count? After all, being busy does not in any way equate to being productive.

Creating Value

A few months ago, a buddy of mine opened a new hotel in Tampa. He'd been working on it for a couple of years and invited me to the grand opening—concert, party, the whole nine yards. I definitely wanted to go because I wanted to support him. And besides, it sounded fun. But at the time, I had a new baby at home.

So I spent the day with my family, hopped a flight and landed in Tampa at six o'clock in the evening, headed to the grand opening party at the hotel and then up to my room an hour later. The entire time I was walking back, however, all I kept thinking about was how my flight was noon the next day and what a waste of time it would be to spend the next twelve hours at a Marriott when I could be with my family. So I opened the app, found a flight, made the ticket change for $350, and booked without hesitation. Zero consideration of cost or exhaustion. All I saw was the colossal waste of time. I may not have slept that night except for a couple of hours on the plane, but I was back home, showered, and made pancakes with my family by eight o'clock in the morning.

I've done that more times than I can count because personally and in business, when you're not creating value, you are losing value. Period. It's very black and white. It's not only just economy of time and trying to fit as much as you can in, but you're also trying to create as much value out of every moment for those things most important to you.

Working efficiently is essential for creating value in a company. Efficient work practices lead to increased productivity, cost savings, and improved quality, all of which contribute to the overall success of any company. When teams complete tasks quickly and effectively, they can get more work done in less time. This increased productivity leads to more goods or services being produced, which can translate into higher revenue and profits. Which also creates time and blank space to do the things only people can do; build relationships with clients.

Not to mention, working efficiently by creating value in every action can help a company save on labor costs, as employees who are able to complete tasks quickly and accurately require less time to complete the same amount of work. I would go so far as to argue that efficiently hustling is a key driver of value creation for a company, and companies that prioritize efficiency can achieve significant benefits in terms of productivity, cost savings, and quality.

But hustling doesn't come without sacrifices. Doing it right means taking time to assess and reflect to make sure the benefits outweigh the costs. And it doesn't always come easy. Hustling is hard. That's why you need to zero in on your *why*. What drives you personally and professionally? Why do you do what you do?

Because without motivation, your hustle won't last long.

Finding Your Motivation

I'm sure you've heard that the most successful people rise early. While it's probably true that many successful people greet the day before everyone else, there's a lot more to it than that. I know a whole lot of people who wake up early and waste a whole lot of time. What gives entrepreneurs their edge isn't their ability to get up early. It's knowing *why* they are driven to do what they do. Which may make them get up early. Which may make them work late. Which may make them fly to Tampa and back within a twelve-hour period.

My list of *whys* is long and deep. For me, family is what makes life worth living. They are my personal *why*. They are the reason I hustle to get back to them, why I hustle at work to do more, to build more, to be better— so I can give them more. My professional *whys* begin with *why the fuck not?* Why can't I build a best-in-class business in a niche industry and dominate it? Which probably originates from some dark place when I was young and someone underestimated my potential. My potential to make a better life, to get the fuck out of my town which had NO opportunity. I knew deep down that I could do every single thing that anyone else could do if I applied myself, including going to college. If they can have it, why can't I? It never even occurred to me that I couldn't have what middle-class families had or that I couldn't be successful.

What gives entrepreneurs their edge isn't their ability to get up early. It's knowing *why* they are driven to do what they do.

I don't push myself beyond my own limits because I'm trying to prove anything to anyone else. I've never been motivated just because someone said I can't do something. My response has been, "I was going to do it anyway, but I'm glad you're here to take notes." Obviously, this response has changed over the years, primarily because of success professionally, having an amazing family, and dollars in the bank. My response now is something like: "I'm not sure exactly why you think you have authority to make a comment like that." This being an expression of my apathy toward them, which usually reinforces that not only do I not care about them but neither do the people closest to them, because putting others down in life is for weak men and women. Or, if feeling especially severe, I take the responsibility of

Robin Hood and kick off a calculated plan to return the favor, which could be years later. Bottom line: I'm motivated by success because I know I can succeed. And I like succeeding. I'm also not ashamed to say that I enjoy the fruits of my labor.

When I have a purpose, I have motivation. And sometimes that purpose comes from a nemesis. Not like a tights-wearing archenemy. Sometimes it's a competitor, but it doesn't always have to be.

Beyond the capital *M* for *Motivation*, for me there's a lowercase *m* that provides the daily fuel to keep hustling: *music*. Loud music. If I want to start my day like a freaking jet engine (which happens four out of five days a week), nothing does it like blasting Led Zeppelin, Rage against the Machine, or Jay-Z's *Black Album*. It's the controlled chaos that gets me charged up. No amount of caffeine in the universe can do that for me. Maybe you've seen athletes before a race, jamming out to whatever song drives their adrenaline, getting all hyped up. That's what gives them that intrinsic spark they need to win. It's the same mentality that's required to focus and consistently compete at a high level.

Imagine if you are the CEO of an InsurTech firm blasting rock and roll so loud that it can be heard in the parking lot as employees are trickling in Monday morning. InsurTech and rock and roll have probably never even been in the same sentence until now. But that's what my team has come to expect and appreciate about my motivation. When they hear the music, they know something is brewing.

Just beware that dwelling too much on a nemesis can be very unhealthy. The nemesis creates the energy like a pilot light. Harness that energy to execute your plan, create your strategic vision, and complete your tasks. Don't give yourself organ failure by internalizing what the other guy is doing. I never pay attention to competitors. Ever. There's no time to troll them. Do your thing, just use the energy (the drive) to do what you need to do to execute. And music is the way for me to harness that energy and focus on doing what needs to be done to define and reach my goals.

Also keep in mind that there are many sacrifices that come with hustling. You will be tired. You won't be able to make everyone happy. You won't always succeed. But you will give yourself the best odds to succeed in all things, including making your business better.

A Fairy Tale about Hustling

Once upon a time, there was a young entrepreneur named Alex. Alex was determined to make it big in the business world and was always on the lookout for opportunities to make money. From a young age, Alex had learned the importance of hustling and was always willing to put in the extra effort to succeed.

Alex started his first business when he was just eighteen years old, and it was a success from the very beginning. He worked tirelessly, putting in long hours and sacrificing his social life to build his business. And his hard work paid off. Within just a few years, Alex had built a thriving company that was the envy of his peers.

But Alex was never satisfied. He always wanted more. So he started another business and then another. He worked even harder, pushing himself to the brink of exhaustion, but he never gave up. And for a while, it seemed like he was invincible.

However, over time, Alex began to neglect the things that were important to him, such as his health, his wife, his friendships, and his happiness. He became so focused on making money that he lost sight of what really mattered in life.

One day, Alex suffered a heart attack. He was rushed to the hospital, but it was too fucking late. His body had been pushed too far, and he passed away shortly after arriving at the hospital. A day after the funeral, his wife married his best friend, and they lived happily ever after.

Alex's story is a tragic reminder of the importance of balance in life. While hustling and working hard are important in business, they should never come at the cost of our health, relationships, and happiness. It's important to work hard, but it's equally important to take care of ourselves and the people we love.

And in the end, it's not the amount of money we make that matters but the impact we have on the people we care about.

Reflections Make You Better

There are many factors that contribute to the success of hustling entrepreneurs. Here are a few reflections from the chapter that may provide clarity on why these hardworking entrepreneurs tend to succeed:

- **Increased Productivity:** When people work hard and hustle, they often achieve more in less time. This increased productivity can lead to higher levels of success, as they are able to accomplish more in their businesses than their peers who may not be as dedicated.

- **More Opportunities:** Entrepreneurs who hustle are often more likely to create and pursue opportunities that others may not see. By working harder and putting in more effort, they may be more likely to find new ways to grow their businesses or to identify gaps in the market that others have overlooked.

- **Improved Resilience:** The journey of an entrepreneur is often a challenging one, filled with setbacks and obstacles. Entrepreneurs who hustle may be better equipped to handle these challenges and bounce back from failures, as they have built up a strong work ethic and a sense of resilience.

- **Stronger Work Ethic:** Entrepreneurs who hustle often have a strong work ethic, which can translate into other areas of their businesses. They may be more diligent about tracking their finances, more focused on customer service, or more dedicated to marketing their products or services.

- **Improved Skill Set:** By putting in more time and effort, entrepreneurs who hustle may also develop stronger skills in areas like sales, marketing, and customer service. This can lead to better results in these areas and, ultimately, greater success.

ELIEVE IN BETTER / THE EVOLUTION OF CORE PRINCIPLES THAT PIONEERED AN INDUSTRY // AUTHENTICITY MAKES OU BETTER // BELIEVE IN BETTER / THE EVOLUTION F CORE PRINCIPLES THAT PIONEERED AN INDUSTRY // USTLING MAKES YOU BETTER // BELIEVE IN BETTER / HE EVOLUTION OF CORE PRINCIPLES THAT PIONEERED AN NDUSTRY // BELIEVE IN BETTER / THE EVOLUTION OF CORE RINCIPLES THAT PIONEERED AN INDUSTRY // SELLING AKES YOU BETTER // BELIEVE IN BETTER / THE EVOLUTION F CORE PRINCIPLES THAT PIONEERED AN INDUSTRY // ELIEVE IN BETTER / THE EVOLUTION OF CORE PRINCIPLES HAT PIONEERED AN INDUSTRY // BELIEVE IN BETTER / HE EVOLUTION OF CORE PRINCIPLES THAT PIONEERED AN NDUSTRY // BELIEVE IN BETTER / THE EVOLUTION OF CORE RINCIPLES THAT PIONEERED AN INDUSTRY // UNDERSTANDING ERSPECTIVE MAKES YOU BETTER //BELIEVE IN BETTER / HE EVOLUTION OF CORE PRINCIPLES THAT PIONEERED AN NDUSTRY // BELIEVE IN BETTER / THE EVOLUTION OF CORE RINCIPLES THAT PIONEERED AN INDUSTRY // TEAMWORK AKES YOU BETTER // BELIEVE IN BETTER / THE EVOLUTION F CORE PRINCIPLES THAT PIONEERED AN INDUSTRY // AKING ACTION MAKES YOU BETTER // BELIEVE IN BETTER THE EVOLUTION OF CORE PRINCIPLES THAT PIONEERED AN NDUSTRY // TRANSPARENCY MAKES YOU BETTER // BELIEVE N BETTER / THE EVOLUTION OF CORE PRINCIPLES THAT IONEERED AN INDUSTRY // DRIVING PROFITABILITY MAKES OU BETTER // THE EVOLUTION OF CORE PRINCIPLES THAT IONEERED AN INDUSTRY // PROCESS MAKES YOU BETTER // ELIEVE IN BETTER / THE EVOLUTION OF CORE PRINCIPLES HAT PIONEERED AN INDUSTRY // CHANGE MAKES YOU BETTER / BELIEVE IN BETTER / THE EVOLUTION OF CORE PRINCIPLE

BELIEVE IN BETTER / THE EVOLUTION OF CORE PRINCIPLES THAT PIONEERED AN INDUSTRY // AUTHENTICITY MAKES YOU BETTER // BELIEVE IN BETTER / THE EVOLUTION OF CORE PRINCIPLES THAT PIONEERED AN INDUSTRY // HUSTLING MAKES YOU BETTER // BELIEVE IN BETTER / THE EVOLUTION OF CORE PRINCIPLES THAT PIONEERED AN INDUSTRY // BELIEVE IN BETTER / THE EVOLUTION OF CORE PRINCIPLES THAT PIONEERED AN INDUSTRY // **SELLING MAKES YOU BETTER** // BELIEVE IN BETTER / THE EVOLUTION OF CORE PRINCIPLES THAT PIONEERED AN INDUSTRY // BELIEVE IN BETTER / THE EVOLUTION OF CORE PRINCIPLES THAT PIONEERED AN INDUSTRY // BELIEVE IN BETTER / THE EVOLUTION OF CORE PRINCIPLES THAT PIONEERED AN INDUSTRY // BELIEVE IN BETTER / THE EVOLUTION OF CORE PRINCIPLES THAT PIONEERED AN INDUSTRY // UNDERSTANDING PERSPECTIVE MAKES YOU BETTER //BELIEVE IN BETTER / THE EVOLUTION OF CORE PRINCIPLES THAT PIONEERED AN INDUSTRY // BELIEVE IN BETTER / THE EVOLUTION OF CORE PRINCIPLES THAT PIONEERED AN INDUSTRY // TEAMWORK MAKES YOU BETTER // BELIEVE IN BETTER / THE EVOLUTION OF CORE PRINCIPLES THAT PIONEERED AN INDUSTRY // TAKING ACTION MAKES YOU BETTER // BELIEVE IN BETTER / THE EVOLUTION OF CORE PRINCIPLES THAT PIONEERED AN INDUSTRY // TRANSPARENCY MAKES YOU BETTER // BELIEVE IN BETTER / THE EVOLUTION OF CORE PRINCIPLES THAT PIONEERED AN INDUSTRY // DRIVING PROFITABILITY MAKES YOU BETTER // THE EVOLUTION OF CORE PRINCIPLES THAT PIONEERED AN INDUSTRY // PROCESS MAKES YOU BETTER // BELIEVE IN BETTER / THE EVOLUTION OF CORE PRINCIPLES THAT PIONEERED AN INDUSTRY // CHANGE MAKES YOU BETTER // BELIEVE IN BETTER / THE EVOLUTION OF CORE PRINCIPLES

Selling Makes You Better

The secret [to selling] is to always let the other man have your way.

—CLAIBORNE PELL

Early in my career, I was asked to man a booth at an industry conference. The company I worked for at the time was a tech company. Back then, I was new to the tech industry and was still trying to familiarize myself with all aspects of it. What I was very familiar with, however, was how freaking lame and ineffective industry conferences were from a sales perspective.

There are so many companies that truly believe they can buy a booth at these conferences and hang all hopes for their sales quota on the random chance that one of the few decent prospects are going to wander by the booth, take a Koozie with the company's logo on it, and strike up a meaningful conversation that leads to an enterprise sale.

Having been in sales for a good part of my life, I can tell you that is *not* an effective strategy. Yet even to this day, it seems to be the norm.

I was more than mortified I had even been talked into manning such a booth. I checked the list of attendees, and sure enough, five out of 2,500 attendees were even remotely a target to sell to. So what did I do? I decided to take a risk and not play along with this asinine strategy. I had literally nothing to lose at that point and thought, "If I'm going to stand in this booth and give shit away all day, I'm at least going to make it memorable."

So, being the immature salesperson that I was, I decided to make a mockery of this ancient game of booth camping. Prior to the event, I went out and bought 1,500 yellow rubber duckies and had our logo printed on them, knowing full well I would need to ask for forgiveness on my expense report. And I didn't even stand at the booth. I just left them out for people to take as they walked by. Within hours, rubber duckies were *everywhere* at the conference. People absolutely loved them. Did that stunt lead to a sale? Nope. Waste of $2,500 on the duckies? Yup! Because it wasn't truly selling. And it definitely was *not* any sort of planned guerilla marketing.

Selling means doing the hard work. Selling is not an event; it's a way of living (much like hustling). Selling in my world means quantifying the value of your product or service to solve a problem. Solve a problem; you create demand. We deliver products and services to our clients with objective facts, allowing them to have the information to make a fair decision promptly, providing a better experience for the policyholder, which can allow their internal operations to run more efficiently because they spend less time getting to the truth. When you are really selling, you're quantifying value across multiple layers in an organization. Too often people want to be the enterprise, white table-cloth salesperson. But real selling is talking to every customer who enters the ice-cream parlor. It's smiling when you scoop out the ice cream for the thousandth time. Things break down in the sales process because people get lazy and don't focus on selling every single individual transaction like it was a $10 million enterprise sale.

Selling is about connecting. It's about educating and influencing. When you think about it, we're *all* salespeople. We're always selling to someone. Our ideas to our team at work. The next vacation to our family. Where to eat for dinner with friends.

People get lazy and don't focus on selling every single individual transaction like it was a $10 million enterprise sale.

I'd even go so far as to say that salespeople—the good ones that is—are influencers of change.

Influencers of Change

I hold selling and people who sell in very high regard. Maybe it's my background, but that's how you could make it in the world. A lot of people frown down on salespeople because of the reputation the bad ones have created with inauthenticity, pushiness, and a lack of transparency. When I rewind all the way back to my college days, the groups that I found myself with all saw selling as a good thing. If you could sell, that meant you could sell yourself. Which meant you'd probably get a good job. Which meant you could close deals and take home big commission checks.

But even more than making money, salespeople can be powerful influencers of change. When they interact with potential customers, they have the ability to highlight the benefits of new products or services, persuading them to embrace innovation and try something new. Salespeople can also act as consultants, offering expert advice and recommendations to clients who may be uncertain about how to implement change in their organization. Through their trust-based relationships with customers, salespeople can identify pain points or areas for improvement and suggest solutions that can help drive positive transformation. When you think about it, salespeople actually play a critical role in shaping the future of a business, driving strategy, and enabling innovation.

The only catch is finding those salespeople worthy of being called influencers of change. When I worked for a healthcare staffing company selling our services to hospitals, I was also responsible for hiring and managing medical recruiters who sold and recruited nuclear med techs, radiology techs, and so on who worked at my branch.

Salespeople actually play a critical role in shaping the future of a business, driving strategy, and enabling innovation.

These medical recruiters were responsible for cold calling all day, identifying and talking to candidates into working for us, validating their credentials, and then negotiating the hourly rate we paid them. Keep in mind when they sold candidates to work with us, we didn't actually have jobs available. And when I sold the hospitals on our resources, we didn't necessarily actually have people who could work there. Talk about selling the ship and figuring out later how to build it!

The medical recruiters' job was to get the best possible candidate for the least amount of money we needed to pay while maintaining quality. When I was running the branch office and took the reins of hiring the recruiters to source candidates, I once implemented a strategy to have an interview where we brought five candidates to a major sporting event and handed each of them $60 cash. Whichever candidate scalped the best seat in the stadium would get the job with us.

The ability to close a deal like that takes a lot of skill sets, but first and foremost, it takes confidence—real or manufactured.

Faking Confidence

When I was twenty-five, I looked like I was eighteen. Today I feel like I'm aging in dog years. There was a time though when I got excited for the gray hairs poking through. Now, not so much. But I digress. When I was first starting out in medical sales in those early days, I remember being interviewed by Elliott Crutchfield, one of the owners of the company I wanted to work for.

"You look like you're twelve," he said. "How are you going to sell to doctors when you look like you should be a pediatric patient?"

"Well, look at you," I replied cooly. "What are you, like thirty? Are you even old enough to own a company?"

Elliott grinned. "You're hired."

That interview could have gone sideways fast. Was I intimidated? Hell yes. Was I confident? Hell no. Did I fake confidence? Hell yes. Once in an interview, comedian Jerry Seinfeld said,[6] "[E]ven to fake [confidence], it's no different from having real confidence." When it comes to selling, and obviously entertainment, that couldn't be more true. You need to stand your ground, straighten your shoulders, and project an air of confidence that you can succeed at anything. Now, that doesn't mean you are arrogant or fail to listen and learn. In fact, you need to intensely and passionately listen. Because even if you are terrified inside, you need to show the outside world *you got this*. Remember, unless you are selling to the International Psychics and

---

6   Jerry Seinfeld, "Steve Martin on Confidence," *Comedians in Cars Getting Coffee*, season 7, episode 2, July 12, 2017, https://www.businessinsider.com/best-career-advice-jerry-seinfeld-comedians-in-cars-getting-coffee-2019-7#steve-martin-on-confidence-season-7-episode-2-3.

Mind Readers Association, no one has any clue what you are thinking. In time, you won't have to fake it because you'll truly know *you got this*.

Selling means doing the work before the sales call or meeting. Know what you are talking about. Selling means not appearing desperate. Nothing kills momentum in selling like a hint of desperation. Your prospect will smell it like cheap cologne. "Sniff, sniff … Is that desperation you are wearing? Oh, it is? I'm not buying."

It means being an expert in your subject matter. It means constantly putting yourself in uncomfortable situations as you grow to the next level. Am I a Hilton? Did I go to Harvard Business School

"Sniff, sniff … Is that desperation you are wearing? Oh, it is? I'm not buying."

or mentor under my dad's chief of staff since the age of seven? No! Believe me, I had no model to follow on how to build a successful, enduring business. I constantly put myself and my team in uncomfortable situations. Was I 100 percent confident we could succeed as we scaled? Hell no. Did my team think I was 100 percent confident we could succeed as we scaled? Hell yes.

Because at the end of the day, nobody is born an expert. Nobody is born competent. And confidence in one thing doesn't necessarily transfer to another discipline. A violinist may be confident as a musician, but as soon as they pick up a tuba, there goes the confidence. Yet with the fundamentals down, a lot of hustle, an openness to learn, and confidence in new skills can emerge in no time.

So when you are selling your business (a.k.a. yourself), you need to sell to *everybody*; your first employee, your second employee, your team, your customers, your partners, your vendors, your friends and family. But how do you sell what you want to so many different people?

With an age-old sales technique.

Make Your Idea *Their* Idea

As chapter two suggested, I'm a huge music fan. So when the opportunity to see the Rolling Stones in concert came up a few years ago, I jumped at it. The fact that the concert was forty-eight hours away and in Prague at an abandoned airfield was just a minor detail I had to navigate.

It was a first-class trip, with a Maybach Mercedes dropping me and my guest off from the hotel at the venue (the Maybach was totally my guest's idea; I would have just Ubered. Probably). Yet when we arrived, there were all these massive security dudes surrounding a European mob all swarming under a pop-up tent, losing their collective minds. None of which was included in the advertising for the event. Was I worried about my safety? Just a little.

Somehow many of the tickets sold were fraudulent. I had purchased our $4,000 worth of tickets through a concierge service, so I was safe, right? Nope. Mine were frauds, too.

As the concert was about to start, I got in line, which wasn't moving. The staff wasn't giving out any wristbands because no one knew who had legitimately purchased tickets and who hadn't. Finally, I made it up to the front. The lady behind the table couldn't have been more than nineteen years old. Thank God, she spoke English, because my Czech was nonexistent. I told her my story as sincerely as possible. "Listen, I know everybody's saying this, but I really did buy these tickets. They cost me $4,000, and I've traveled so far to get here. I understand if you can't do it, but if you could walk over to that box of wristbands (I pointed in a low-key way so nobody would see me, sort of under my hand), take two and put them in my hand, I will walk away without saying a word, and you will know you have done the right thing."

She looked at me for a second, and then she walked over and put two wristbands in my hand. I thanked her profusely (and softly, so the giant Turkish dudes wouldn't overhear), and moments later, my guest and I were in the pit section staring up at Keith Richards from the second row. How was I able to pull off such an unbelievable move? Because I tapped into her humanness.

After all, it's human nature to want to help one another. I could have yelled and stomped and cussed her out, which would have gotten me nowhere. But when I presented her with an option to do something that was in her nature, to help a fellow human being, she took ownership. My idea had become her idea, and she felt good about herself by doing the right thing.

By presenting your idea in a way that aligns with the other person's goals, values, or interests, the other person is more likely to see the idea as their own and become more invested in it. For example, if you want to persuade a coworker to work on a project with you, you could highlight how it aligns with their career goals and how it would benefit their professional development. By framing it this way, you are making the idea of working on the project together their own, which can increase their motivation and commitment to it.

Notice in the last couple of examples how selling didn't look anything like selling. Author and screenwriter Elmore Leonard said it best: "If it sounds like writing … rewrite it." The same applies to selling. When selling feels like selling, it's going to fail.

That's why at my company, we don't sell. We educate.

Educate, Don't Sell

But before you even earn the right to educate a prospect, you must be credible. You need to build trust as they do their due diligence vetting you. Then when they open that email or answer the phone, it's game on. The second you become a salesperson, however, it's over. Our philosophy is to *only* sell through education—to do the hard work, not just pick up the phone and ask for revenue or waste our customers' precious time telling them that we have resources available for them. Because guess what

When selling feels like selling, it's going to fail.

happens next time you call? Nothing. You lose credibility because you are just another salesperson calling in to hock your goods.

We educate them on complicated subject matters at a high level, giving them enough information to do their job a little easier. In the education sessions, without even having to say it, they get how terribly complex our role can be, which highlights the value we provide when they buy our products and services. Ultimately, they see us as the expert they can't live without.

Our educational seminars are the size of small concerts—four thousand people registered for an hour's worth of insurance claim discussions. Think about that. *Insurance claims*, not coffee talk with Eddie Vedder. But it happens because educating helps to reinforce trust and credibility, as it shows that you are more concerned with helping customers and prospects make an informed decision rather than just making a sale. It also helps to create a long-term relationship with the buyer, as they are more likely to come back to you for future purchases if they feel that you have their best interests in mind.

Second, educating a buyer can lead to more informed decision-making. When buyers understand the benefits and drawbacks of different products or services, they are better able to make a decision that meets their needs and preferences. This can lead to greater satisfaction with their purchase, which can, in turn, lead to positive reviews and referrals. Think about it this way: Are you more likely to trust the surgeon who runs through the pros and cons of a particular surgery or one who blows off your questions and tells you to trust the process?

Educating a buyer can lead to more informed decision-making.

I don't know about you, but the first surgeon gets all my lobotomy business.

Finally, educating a buyer can differentiate you from competitors who have no business being employed, much less hold the prestigious title of salesperson. By demonstrating your expertise and commitment to helping buyers make informed decisions, you can stand out from the crowd and establish yourself as a trusted advisor in your industry.

A Fairy Tale about Selling

Once upon a time, there was a young man named Jack who dreamed of becoming a successful businessman selling apples. He had heard stories of wealthy merchants and traders who had made their fortunes through their skills in selling. So one day Jack decided to set out on a journey to learn the secrets of successful selling.

He walked for days and nights, asking merchants and traders for advice, but nobody seemed to have a clear answer. Some said it was all about having the right product, while others said it was about knowing the right people. But they all mentioned a mysterious old man on a faraway road who had no competition in selling apples. He was the best. Jack went out and spent weeks in search of him.

Finally, Jack came across the old man who was sitting by the side of the road, selling his apples. Jack told the old man that he, too, sold apples and asked what his secret was to selling so many apples. The old man smiled and said, "Because mine are magical. Anyone who eats them will instantly become the best salesperson in the world."

Jack immediately bought an apple from the old man and started eating. Suddenly he felt sick. The old man laughed devilishly. Jack knew he had been tricked, but it was too fucking late. Jack shuddered, fell to the ground, and died right then and there.

What Jack didn't understand was that selling is not just about having a good product or knowing the right people, but it is about being able to convince people that they need what you have to offer. Did Jack need an apple? No, he had plenty of his own. But the old man, wanting to eliminate the competition, made Jack *think* he needed one of his magical apples.

Jack had been looking for the secret to selling in all the wrong places. And he failed to recognize the double-edged power of persuasion. The moral of the story? Beware of being outsold by a salesperson more savvy than you.

Reflections Make You Better

Here are five tips for leveraging selling to make your business better:

- **Know Your Audience:** To effectively sell, you need to understand the needs, wants, and values of your audience. Take the time to research and understand your target market and tailor your messaging accordingly.

- **Build Trust:** Trust is an essential element in any successful business relationship. Build trust with your audience by being honest, being transparent, and delivering on your promises.

- **Tell a Story:** People are more likely to remember and connect with stories than with facts and figures. Use storytelling to capture your audience's attention and create an emotional connection with them.

- **Create a Sense of Urgency:** Creating a sense of urgency can motivate your audience to take action. Use time-limited offers, or highlight the potential consequences of not taking action to create a sense of urgency. In some cases, you need to put the buyer in a position to make a decision, and then illustrate the different paths' outcomes based on the decision they make. Master the art of reverse selling, and rule the universe.

- **Use Social Proof:** People are more likely to be persuaded by the actions of others than by what they are told. Use social proof, such as customer testimonials or case studies, to demonstrate the value of your products or services and build trust with your audience. Being the early adopter can be scary for some; the safety of others and pressure of not being left behind is a powerful tactic.

ELIEVE IN BETTER / THE EVOLUTION OF CORE PRINCIPLES
HAT PIONEERED AN INDUSTRY // AUTHENTICITY MAKES
OU BETTER // BELIEVE IN BETTER / THE EVOLUTION
F CORE PRINCIPLES THAT PIONEERED AN INDUSTRY //
USTLING MAKES YOU BETTER // BELIEVE IN BETTER /
HE EVOLUTION OF CORE PRINCIPLES THAT PIONEERED AN
NDUSTRY // BELIEVE IN BETTER / THE EVOLUTION OF CORE
RINCIPLES THAT PIONEERED AN INDUSTRY // SELLING
AKES YOU BETTER // BELIEVE IN BETTER / THE EVOLUTION
F CORE PRINCIPLES THAT PIONEERED AN INDUSTRY //
ELIEVE IN BETTER / THE EVOLUTION OF CORE PRINCIPLES
HAT PIONEERED AN INDUSTRY // BELIEVE IN BETTER /
HE EVOLUTION OF CORE PRINCIPLES THAT PIONEERED AN
NDUSTRY // BELIEVE IN BETTER / THE EVOLUTION OF CORE
RINCIPLES THAT PIONEERED AN INDUSTRY // UNDERSTANDING
ERSPECTIVE MAKES YOU BETTER //BELIEVE IN BETTER /
HE EVOLUTION OF CORE PRINCIPLES THAT PIONEERED AN
NDUSTRY // BELIEVE IN BETTER / THE EVOLUTION OF CORE
RINCIPLES THAT PIONEERED AN INDUSTRY // TEAMWORK
AKES YOU BETTER // BELIEVE IN BETTER / THE EVOLUTION
F CORE PRINCIPLES THAT PIONEERED AN INDUSTRY //
AKING ACTION MAKES YOU BETTER // BELIEVE IN BETTER
 THE EVOLUTION OF CORE PRINCIPLES THAT PIONEERED AN
NDUSTRY // TRANSPARENCY MAKES YOU BETTER // BELIEVE
N BETTER / THE EVOLUTION OF CORE PRINCIPLES THAT
IONEERED AN INDUSTRY // DRIVING PROFITABILITY MAKES
OU BETTER // THE EVOLUTION OF CORE PRINCIPLES THAT
IONEERED AN INDUSTRY // PROCESS MAKES YOU BETTER //
ELIEVE IN BETTER / THE EVOLUTION OF CORE PRINCIPLES
HAT PIONEERED AN INDUSTRY // CHANGE MAKES YOU BETTER
/ BELIEVE IN BETTER / THE EVOLUTION OF CORE PRINCIPLE

BELIEVE IN BETTER / THE EVOLUTION OF CORE PRINCIPLE THAT PIONEERED AN INDUSTRY // AUTHENTICITY MAKE YOU BETTER // BELIEVE IN BETTER / THE EVOLUTIO OF CORE PRINCIPLES THAT PIONEERED AN INDUSTRY / HUSTLING MAKES YOU BETTER // BELIEVE IN BETTER THE EVOLUTION OF CORE PRINCIPLES THAT PIONEERED A INDUSTRY // BELIEVE IN BETTER / THE EVOLUTION OF COR PRINCIPLES THAT PIONEERED AN INDUSTRY // SELLIN MAKES YOU BETTER // BELIEVE IN BETTER / THE EVOLUTIO OF CORE PRINCIPLES THAT PIONEERED AN INDUSTRY / BELIEVE IN BETTER / THE EVOLUTION OF CORE PRINCIPLE THAT PIONEERED AN INDUSTRY // BELIEVE IN BETTER THE EVOLUTION OF CORE PRINCIPLES THAT PIONEERED A INDUSTRY // BELIEVE IN BETTER / THE EVOLUTION OF COR PRINCIPLES THAT PIONEERED AN INDUSTRY // **UNDERSTANDIN PERSPECTIVE MAKES YOU BETTER** //BELIEVE IN BETTER THE EVOLUTION OF CORE PRINCIPLES THAT PIONEERED A INDUSTRY // BELIEVE IN BETTER / THE EVOLUTION OF COR PRINCIPLES THAT PIONEERED AN INDUSTRY // TEAMWOR MAKES YOU BETTER // BELIEVE IN BETTER / THE EVOLUTIO OF CORE PRINCIPLES THAT PIONEERED AN INDUSTRY / TAKING ACTION MAKES YOU BETTER // BELIEVE IN BETTE / THE EVOLUTION OF CORE PRINCIPLES THAT PIONEERED A INDUSTRY // TRANSPARENCY MAKES YOU BETTER // BELIEV IN BETTER / THE EVOLUTION OF CORE PRINCIPLES THA PIONEERED AN INDUSTRY // DRIVING PROFITABILITY MAKE YOU BETTER // THE EVOLUTION OF CORE PRINCIPLES THA PIONEERED AN INDUSTRY // PROCESS MAKES YOU BETTER / BELIEVE IN BETTER / THE EVOLUTION OF CORE PRINCIPLE THAT PIONEERED AN INDUSTRY // CHANGE MAKES YOU BETTE // BELIEVE IN BETTER / THE EVOLUTION OF CORE PRINCIPL

Understanding Perspective Makes You Better

Some people see the glass half full. Others see it half empty.
I see a glass that's twice as big as it needs to be.

—GEORGE CARLIN

When I started my company in 2011, a low budget way to gain credibility was to write press releases. For $200 to $300, we could submit them through a PR newswire service where they would get distributed to all sorts of media outlets. It goes without saying that these articles were little more than glorified opinion pieces, as most press releases are. But they served to establish us as thought leaders on all sorts of subject matter, which gave us an edge by showcasing significant educational content when insurance carriers came across them. And, of course, we'd have a shameless plug at the end, pushing our service as HVAC investigators.

In one particular article, I covered the rules and regulations of R22 refrigerant. For the uninitiated, this is one of the substances used in air-conditioning units to cool your home or office. There are very specific Environmental Protection Agency (EPA) guidelines in place regarding R22 because of the potential of it affecting the atmosphere if it isn't handled properly. This issue has only become more complex over the years. And the more complex those regulations get, the better it is for our company, as insurance carriers look to us for insight and answers.

Those were the days when we worked out of the very unimpressive, fluorescent-lit office that looked like we borrowed it from a 1970s dentist and forgot to give it back. It was late morning when one of our team members let me know that I had a call on line two—a whole three hours after I put out the press release and eight months into me even knowing what R22 was.

"Who is it?" I asked.

"The EPA," they said.

Little more to say at that point except, "Shit."

I was hardly an expert, but at least I had done my research and pulled together several credible sources for the article, including contracting with HVAC experts who provided guidance on this highly regulated topic. It was amazing to discover that all the answers to this controversial issue were right there on the EPA website. You just had to actually read the EPA documents and open the links to understand the rules. Go figure. But no matter how prepared you think you are, at the end of the day, the EPA calling is a lot like the Internal Revenue Service (IRS) calling. It's never a social call.

I swallowed hard and picked up the line. "Good morning, this is Damon."

"Hi, this is John from the EPA in Washington, DC," he said very officially. "I sit on the congressional committee for refrigerant change policies and also happen to be responsible for all communications regarding the subject. I noticed you posted a press release on R22. Can you look at paragraph two, sentence three and clarify your statement on ..."

I was terrified. But while he spoke, I remember having a Kevin McCallister moment from *Home Alone* and thinking, "I have the EPA on the line! *The* authority on everything my business is built upon. This is an opportunity to either crash and burn or win him over and develop an incredible ally."

I kicked right into sales mode. "Sure, I'm happy to help. Let me go through this paragraph with you ..."

We went through my quote, and I immediately started building a relationship with the freaking EPA. As the be-all and end-all for these regulations, I invited him to offer feedback and insight. It turned out to be a fantastic call. Fast-forward a few years later, I received the following email:

Dear Stakeholder,

The U.S. Environmental Protection Agency (EPA) Office of Atmospheric Programs announces a public meeting to gather individual input from members of the public on the potential for extending Clean Air Act (CAA) section 608 regulations to substitutes for ozone-depleting substances (ODS). On September 16, 2014, EPA announced that it would engage stakeholders to identify refrigerant management options to

reduce hydrofluorocarbon (HFC) emissions from
air conditioning and refrigeration equipment.
The public meeting being held on November 12,
2014, will begin this process of stakeholder
engagement. The primary purpose of the meeting
will be to solicit ideas to reduce emissions
of both high global warming potential (GWP)
substitute refrigerants, such as HFCs, as well
as ozone-depleting refrigerants, with a focus
on emissions during the service, maintenance,
repair and disposal of air conditioning and
refrigeration appliances.

WHEN: The public meeting will begin at 9 a.m.
ET on November 12, 2014.

WHERE: The meeting will be held at Twelve &
K Hotel, 1201 K Street, NW, Washington, DC
20005.

PARTICIPATION: RSVP by November 5, 2014, if
you plan to attend the meeting.

He actually invited us to join the stakeholder committee for making multibillion-dollar refrigerant decisions. A year later, my company was in Washington, DC, sitting at the table where opinions were heard, where information was gathered and used to make decisions. We were even asked to provide data that they used to make future decisions. Talk about feeling influential.

What if I had blown off John from the EPA when he called? What if I had dodged him? Or become defensive and obnoxious? From his perspective, he was calling what he believed to be a fellow expert in his field. He liked what I had to say and was looking for an alliance.

From my perspective, I wasn't an expert. Yet. But I had leaned on the data and followed the research of experts. And by embracing John's perspective of me, I went from being an outsider to sitting around a committee table with stakeholders who were closer than anyone to major environmental and economic decisions that impact an industry in the tens of billions.

In business, sometimes we need to see things through others' eyes. That could be the eyes of our customers, our colleagues, or even our competitors. Perspective, by definition, is relative to the beholder. It's never easy to see the world from another point of view, but it's critical for enduring success.

See the World through Their Eyes

We had a new partner years ago who closed a $300,000 order for our company. Having worked the deal all on his own, he knew all the numbers—how much the deal was worth to the business, what the profit margin was, and so forth. One of our other partners at the time wanted to really show him how much the company appreciated his efforts, so he rewarded him with a set of Bose headphones. No bonus, no special recognition, no promise of all expense paid vacation, nothing. This former partner had zero clue what sort of reward would have been appropriate for landing such a large deal. He lacked the ability to see the

Leadership in any business requires the ability to see things through another's perspective.

world through another's eyes and truly believed a set of headphones was an adequate thank-you. We still joke at our monthly meetings about those Bose headphones being one of the most offensive gifts in history.

Leadership in any business requires the ability to see things through another's perspective. What we're really talking about here is emotional intelligence or emotional quotient (EI or EQ), the social and psychological equivalent of IQ. EQ refers to a person's ability to identify, understand, and manage their own emotions, as well as the emotions of others.

The components that make up EQ include the following:

Self-awareness: This is the ability to recognize and understand your own emotions and how they affect your thoughts and behaviors.

Self-regulation: This is the ability to control your own emotions and behaviors and to adapt to changing circumstances.

Motivation: This is the ability to use your emotions to drive you toward achieving your goals.

Empathy: This is the ability to understand and relate to the emotions of others and to respond appropriately.

Social Skills: This is the ability to communicate effectively with others, build relationships, and work collaboratively.

EQ is a key factor in determining an individual's success in both personal and professional settings. And it is especially important for leadership. Not being able to read the room, pick up on unhappy or disengaged teammates, reward and recognize achievements appropriately, or communicate clearly and professionally will impact the success of the leader and the business.

Understanding the perspective of others doesn't mean reading their minds but reading the signs.

One thing that really gets on my nerves is what I call Country Club Syndrome. This is a phenomenon that occurs in some professionals when they are unwaveringly locked into a lifestyle that they assume everyone has or desires—the military-grade SUV to take the kids to school or soccer practice (G-Wagon), the best neighborhood, the biggest house on the block, and, as the name suggests, membership to an exclusive country club. But the syndrome goes even deeper, as those who suffer from it talk about a *burn rate*, which is the cost of living to have such a lifestyle, which they—without question—deserve more than anyone else, which means their team, their employer, better meet their financial goals so the lifestyle can continue. All decisions are made through this lens, shortsighted at best, and an odorous vibe of entitlement that bubbles up from their caramel-raspberry latte with three pumps-no-whip-with-oat milk-soaked bowels.

As a manager or team lead or owner of the company, how does that sort of perspective affect the team at large? What does that say about their team's lifestyles, which may very likely be at a different level?

As a leader, you'd better be able to exercise a little EQ and read the room before complaining about the ongoing remodeling project in the west wing of the country club. The fact is, nobody gives a shit. All you end up doing is building resentment and sowing the seeds of disharmony. I'm not saying that belonging to a country club or living in a certain neighborhood or driving an expensive car is wrong. I may very well do all those things. But I don't have to make sure everyone at work knows about it.

When we can open our hearts and minds to new perspectives, it allows us to expand our understanding of the world and the people in it and reframe the level of douchebaggery your statement could create.

Welcome New Perspectives

At one of our service brands within Alpine Intel, we consider the perspective on the fundamentals of how HVAC equipment works from experts in the field, from the manufacturers, and from the service technicians. Then we consider the perspective of the insurance carrier to understand what they truly need to make a fair decision to take care of their policyholder who is in need. On top of that, we go to the EPA, and we seek to understand their perspective on what exactly the rules are for the subject matter. All of these perspectives aggregate into the nucleus of our perspective, which represents the value of the product that we deliver. Not to mention, this intersection of information that creates value for our customers also creates *tremendous* value for our shareholders.

In business, it's easy to get lost in an echo chamber and simply see the world from one perspective. The key is to surround yourself with people who are aligned with you, not those who necessarily agree with you. This is how you create productive friction, the essence that drives forward momentum to accomplish goals.

Surround yourself with people who are aligned with you, not those who necessarily agree with you.

When you think of a military operation, for instance, there are several stakeholders involved who need to weigh in. The general back at the Pentagon is always considering the political implications of the operation. The field operatives are literally in the trenches, making immediate decisions to stay alive and complete the mission. But they can't see what the Blackhawk helicopter pilot with night vision can see from the air—that an ambush lies in wait across the river.

By considering different viewpoints, we can gain insight into how others think, feel, and experience life, which can increase our empathy and ability to relate to others. In addition, it can help us to become more creative and innovative, as we are able to draw on a wider range of ideas and experiences. Opening our minds to new perspectives can also improve our problem-solving abilities, as we are able to approach challenges from a broader range of angles. Finally, it can be incredibly enriching and rewarding to learn about new cultures, traditions, and ways of life.

But for perspectives to really be useful, they can't remain static for long.

Perspective Needs to Evolve

The best product I've ever created needed to be trashed after two grueling years and a $30-plus million investment. This was—from my perspective—one of those perfect silver bullets that provided our customers exactly what they needed to translate data into information, so they could take action and influence the change needed to significantly drive more profitability and take policyholder market share from their competitors.

Opening our minds to new perspectives can also improve our problem-solving abilities.

The platform worked great and provided an even bigger outcome than expected. Yet within the development period, the world had changed. A certain pandemic you may have heard of swept across the business landscape, changing perspectives in its wake. Without getting into the weeds too deeply, the product I created solved one of the biggest problems we had ever been presented in insurance. But it didn't take into account the macro decisions that would have needed to be made under strained economic conditions, which would have led to teams of people being eliminated. And when the economy is struggling, insurance carriers want to write as many new policies as possible, even if it costs them revenue. At that point it's about market share, which my platform didn't take into consideration.

Yes, my new product solved a major problem but only under the right conditions. The conditions I was familiar with. COVID-19 changed that, and so my perspective needed to evolve as the world changed.

Up until that point, I was the living incarnation of the hockey stick curve to my investors. Every problem we'd been handed still allowed us to grow "up and to the right." Now I had to tell them we needed to pull the plug on the eighteen-month project to stop the bleeding. It was one of the most difficult decisions I've ever had to make, but that's what we did. I stood in front of our board and laid out the situation. Over a few meetings, we covered all the nuances of the project and the decision to scrap it based on the new business landscape. But I have the best investors a CEO could ask for. They were incredibly supportive and measured the opportunity costs of other things we could focus on. Which incidentally, two months later, allowed us the time, resources, and attention to land the cliché "transformative" deal, which at the time was our biggest and most profitable deal.

Any good rock climber will tell you, sometimes you need to let go of the rock you are holding on to to reach the summit.

Had we tried to ride out the lost cause, we may not have had the bandwidth to entertain that deal. But by evolving my perspective, I was able to more objectively assess what was best for the business, not my ego. Any good rock climber will tell you, sometimes you need to let go of the rock you are holding on to—and even climb downward—to reach the summit.

Perspective is relative, but it is also dynamic. In order to remain relevant and successful, your perspective needs to evolve and adapt to changing circumstances and new information. One key aspect of maintaining a dynamic perspective in business is to understand that maybe somebody else does it better or has a great idea or approach. This has to be paired with a quick evaluation and go/no go decision, however, or you will drown in others' thoughts. The point is, don't get stuck in old ways of thinking or doing things just because they've worked in the past. Be willing to explore new ideas, experiment with different approaches, and embrace change.

It's also crucial to be willing to learn from your mistakes and failures. Pulling the plug on a failed project gave me the greatest confidence I could have when making decisions on acquisitions, measuring opportunity costs, and generally honing my strategic decision-making skills. It's hard to think about the big picture when you are in the weeds, giving every ounce of sweat in your body to make something successful.

By maintaining a dynamic perspective, you'll be better equipped to navigate the challenges and opportunities that come your way.

So don't let setbacks discourage you or cause you to give up on your goals. Instead, use them as opportunities to learn and grow *and* to refine your perspective and approach.

Remember, perspective is not a one-time thing. It requires ongoing attention, reflection, and refinement. By maintaining a dynamic perspective, you'll be better equipped to navigate the challenges and opportunities that come your way and to achieve success in business.

Take it from me. I had to evolve my perspective many times throughout my life. I started from the very bottom, born in Gastonia, North Carolina. Never heard of Gastonia? Home of Sun Drop, Big Game James (James Worthy), Sleepy Floyd, and HV3. Where the adolescent years were spent for the frontman for Limp Bizkit, and the screenwriter who came up with "Yippy Ki YaY, Mother Fucker" for Bruce Willis in Die Hard. Gastonia, or as it's notoriously referred to as The Gashouse, has an underlying seedy element that makes it strangely endearing to call home. People called it Little Chicago in the 80s because of the capital murder rate and crime. People from Charlotte avoided it, unless they were bravely making a trek to Mary Jo's for fabric or a Sun Drop slushy at the Handy Pantry on RedBud. Boys 2 Men once performed in Gastonia at the Fish Camp Jam, where people celebrated the town's connection to fried seafood and literally raced live catfish in tanks, only to have their performance interrupted by the sound of gunfire (later claimed to be fireworks) and an ensuing riot. It's safe to say they're never coming back. Don't get me wrong: there are some incredible people and some great parts of Gastonia, but it wasn't the ideal place to be brought into as a kid.

I grew up in the mountains, and there were times where we were eating only what we grew in the garden. I had to change my perspective to make sure my life kept on that "up and to the right" trajectory. And for somebody who has started from nothing, it's even harder to take failure. But failure is an amazing teacher if you have the courage to listen.

A Fairy Tale about Perspective

Once upon a time, there was a business owner named Mabel. She had a successful clothing store in a bustling town, but she always felt like she could do better. Mabel was always searching for new ways to improve her business, but no matter how hard she tried, she couldn't seem to make any progress.

One day, while on a trip to a remote village, Mabel stumbled upon a group of weavers who were creating the most beautiful fabrics she had ever seen—corduroy. She immediately saw an opportunity to bring these fabrics to her store and increase her profits.

Excited by her discovery, Mabel made a deal with the weavers to purchase their fabrics and bring them to the city. She knew that her customers would love the unique designs and exquisite quality of the corduroy. She made corduroy shirts, scarves, socks, hats, T-shirts, and underwear.

But when Mabel reopened her store, she was shocked by the lack of interest in the new clothing line. Her customers seemed indifferent to the new designs, and sales were slow. Mabel was puzzled and frustrated, unable to understand why her plan had failed.

One day, while sitting in her store, Mabel overheard two customers talking. They were admiring the clothing, but one of them said, "I wish these corduroys were made by local artisans. It would be great to support our corduroy community."

Mabel had never thought about it that way. She had been so focused on profits and expanding her business that she hadn't considered the perspective of her customers. Mabel had lost sight of the bigger picture.

Determined to make things right, Mabel decided to change her approach. She started working with local artisans to create new corduroy designs that would appeal to her customers. But it was too fucking late.

One night, a group of masked locals torched her workshop with her in it. Mabel and her corduroy clothing line were burnt to a crisp. The next day, the customers whom Mabel had overheard talking in her store launched a new clothing shop that supported the local community. The store became known for its unique and locally sourced corduroy, and the business grew stronger than anyone ever expected. Those owners understood that perspective was key to success in business and that the best way to achieve their goals was by working with, not against, the corduroy community.

Reflections Make You Better

In business, perspective is a key driver of success. Entrepreneurs who take a broad view of the market and consider multiple perspectives are better equipped to identify new opportunities, make informed decisions, and build strong relationships with their employees, customers, and other stakeholders. By valuing diversity and practicing empathy, entrepreneurs can build a more sustainable business that is better equipped to weather challenges and adapt to changing circumstances. Here are five tips on how perspective can make entrepreneurs better in business:

- **See Things from the Customer's Perspective:** People who take the time to understand their customers' needs and wants can create products and services that solve problems, therefore creating tangible value and leading to increased customer satisfaction and loyalty. Understanding the perspective of the customer can also help entrepreneurs create more effective returns on investments and develop stronger relationships with their target audience.

- **Take a Holistic View:** It's important to consider the broader impact of their business, not just the bottom line. Taking a holistic view means considering the social, environmental, and economic impact of their business and making decisions that benefit all stakeholders. This perspective can help build a more sustainable and resilient business over the long term.

- **Embrace Diversity:** Entrepreneurs who value diversity and seek out diverse perspectives can benefit from a wider range of ideas and insights. This can lead to more creative solutions to problems, more effective marketing strategies, and a stronger understanding of different customer segments. Embracing diversity can also create a more inclusive workplace culture, which can attract and retain top talent.

- **Force Long-Term Thinking:** Entrepreneurs who take a long-term perspective are better able to anticipate future challenges and opportunities. By focusing on the big picture, they can make decisions that create sustainable growth and build resilience against economic downturns or other challenges. A long-term perspective can also help entrepreneurs build a strong reputation and brand identity over time.

- **Practice Empathy:** Entrepreneurs who practice empathy are better able to understand the needs and motivations of their employees, customers, and other stakeholders. By putting themselves in others' shoes, they can build stronger relationships and create a more positive work environment. Empathy can also help develop more effective leadership skills and inspire loyalty and commitment from their team.

BELIEVE IN BETTER / THE EVOLUTION OF CORE PRINCIPLES THAT PIONEERED AN INDUSTRY // AUTHENTICITY MAKES YOU BETTER // BELIEVE IN BETTER / THE EVOLUTION OF CORE PRINCIPLES THAT PIONEERED AN INDUSTRY // HUSTLING MAKES YOU BETTER // BELIEVE IN BETTER / THE EVOLUTION OF CORE PRINCIPLES THAT PIONEERED AN INDUSTRY // BELIEVE IN BETTER / THE EVOLUTION OF CORE PRINCIPLES THAT PIONEERED AN INDUSTRY // SELLING MAKES YOU BETTER // BELIEVE IN BETTER / THE EVOLUTION OF CORE PRINCIPLES THAT PIONEERED AN INDUSTRY // BELIEVE IN BETTER / THE EVOLUTION OF CORE PRINCIPLES THAT PIONEERED AN INDUSTRY // BELIEVE IN BETTER / THE EVOLUTION OF CORE PRINCIPLES THAT PIONEERED AN INDUSTRY // BELIEVE IN BETTER / THE EVOLUTION OF CORE PRINCIPLES THAT PIONEERED AN INDUSTRY // UNDERSTANDING PERSPECTIVE MAKES YOU BETTER //BELIEVE IN BETTER / THE EVOLUTION OF CORE PRINCIPLES THAT PIONEERED AN INDUSTRY // BELIEVE IN BETTER / THE EVOLUTION OF CORE PRINCIPLES THAT PIONEERED AN INDUSTRY // TEAMWORK MAKES YOU BETTER // BELIEVE IN BETTER / THE EVOLUTION OF CORE PRINCIPLES THAT PIONEERED AN INDUSTRY // TAKING ACTION MAKES YOU BETTER // BELIEVE IN BETTER / THE EVOLUTION OF CORE PRINCIPLES THAT PIONEERED AN INDUSTRY // TRANSPARENCY MAKES YOU BETTER // BELIEVE IN BETTER / THE EVOLUTION OF CORE PRINCIPLES THAT PIONEERED AN INDUSTRY // DRIVING PROFITABILITY MAKES YOU BETTER // THE EVOLUTION OF CORE PRINCIPLES THAT PIONEERED AN INDUSTRY // PROCESS MAKES YOU BETTER // BELIEVE IN BETTER / THE EVOLUTION OF CORE PRINCIPLES THAT PIONEERED AN INDUSTRY // CHANGE MAKES YOU BETTER // BELIEVE IN BETTER / THE EVOLUTION OF CORE PRINCIPLE

BELIEVE IN BETTER / THE EVOLUTION OF CORE PRINCIPLES THAT PIONEERED AN INDUSTRY // AUTHENTICITY MAKES YOU BETTER // BELIEVE IN BETTER / THE EVOLUTION OF CORE PRINCIPLES THAT PIONEERED AN INDUSTRY // HUSTLING MAKES YOU BETTER // BELIEVE IN BETTER / THE EVOLUTION OF CORE PRINCIPLES THAT PIONEERED AN INDUSTRY // BELIEVE IN BETTER / THE EVOLUTION OF CORE PRINCIPLES THAT PIONEERED AN INDUSTRY // SELLING MAKES YOU BETTER // BELIEVE IN BETTER / THE EVOLUTION OF CORE PRINCIPLES THAT PIONEERED AN INDUSTRY // BELIEVE IN BETTER / THE EVOLUTION OF CORE PRINCIPLES THAT PIONEERED AN INDUSTRY // BELIEVE IN BETTER / THE EVOLUTION OF CORE PRINCIPLES THAT PIONEERED AN INDUSTRY // BELIEVE IN BETTER / THE EVOLUTION OF CORE PRINCIPLES THAT PIONEERED AN INDUSTRY // UNDERSTANDING PERSPECTIVE MAKES YOU BETTER //BELIEVE IN BETTER / THE EVOLUTION OF CORE PRINCIPLES THAT PIONEERED AN INDUSTRY // BELIEVE IN BETTER / THE EVOLUTION OF CORE PRINCIPLES THAT PIONEERED AN INDUSTRY // **TEAMWORK MAKES YOU BETTER** // BELIEVE IN BETTER / THE EVOLUTION OF CORE PRINCIPLES THAT PIONEERED AN INDUSTRY // TAKING ACTION MAKES YOU BETTER // BELIEVE IN BETTER / THE EVOLUTION OF CORE PRINCIPLES THAT PIONEERED AN INDUSTRY // TRANSPARENCY MAKES YOU BETTER // BELIEVE IN BETTER / THE EVOLUTION OF CORE PRINCIPLES THAT PIONEERED AN INDUSTRY // DRIVING PROFITABILITY MAKES YOU BETTER // THE EVOLUTION OF CORE PRINCIPLES THAT PIONEERED AN INDUSTRY // PROCESS MAKES YOU BETTER // BELIEVE IN BETTER / THE EVOLUTION OF CORE PRINCIPLES THAT PIONEERED AN INDUSTRY // CHANGE MAKES YOU BETTER // BELIEVE IN BETTER / THE EVOLUTION OF CORE PRINCIPLES

05

Teamwork Makes You Better

Coming together is a beginning. Keeping together is progress.
Working together is success.

—HENRY FORD

At Alpine Intel, we have a company scoreboard that everyone has access to. We can see which individuals are hitting their Key Performance Indicators (KPIs) while maintaining full transparency into how each team is tracking toward company goals. No one ever calls me to crow about how a line of business performed last week because I already have access to the data. In fact, I get an automated text if someone drops below pacing for a particular goal. However, I also get a text when someone knocks it out of the park.

This level of transparency also generates a fair amount of healthy competition among departments because just like each team member has specific goals, each team has specific goals. And within teams are sub-teams striving toward their own goals. Last year at one of our quarterly meetings, our CRO shoved the game ball in our COO's face because the sales team blew their goals out of the water and stressed operations to a point where they had to work around the clock.

But give it time, and operations will eventually say, "Hey, what's going on, sales team? You guys just playing golf? We're twiddling our thumbs over here." Real collaboration and productivity require friction. And as any good physicist will tell you, "friction creates traction."

I'm of the mind that people are inherently self-serving, and I mean that in a good way, not necessarily a selfish way. They care about how the outcome or goal affects them first and foremost. The most successful teams we've ever created are made up of people who are incentivized to achieve individual goals, not necessarily team goals. Achieving team goals and thereby company goals is the desired outcome, but I've found the more we incentivize individual performance, the more success we have at mapping that across all other goals. This seems counterintuitive to the common collaboration and kumbaya in business, the all-for-one and one-for-all clichés you might find in other business books. In all honesty, the greatest progress we've made as a company is incenting leaders of the company (for those financially coin operated) to things that they can influence.

This presents a surprising conflict between investor relationships and those driving growth within the business. Everyone wants a simple compensation model and simple incentive plan that we can all understand, tied to the profitability of the company. But you can't get anything done that way. Allow me to elaborate: Let's say an operational manager has a personal incentive of half of their bonus being tied to output and profitability. If you set up the incentive where exceeding their goal by 25 percent means a 200 percent increase to that bonus, you've just covered the delta for the rest of the team. That basically ensures that team goals are met.

Bottom line, stretch bonuses and incentives that "pay for themselves" through company profitability are healthy for everyone and mitigate the risk of underperformance of other areas of the business.

Now, with all that said about teams and how critical they are in the success of the company, I'm also the guy who rolls his eyes when people describe their business as having a "team environment full of like-minded agreement and harmony." Harmony does not translate to success in business. It's code speak for "not getting shit done." And the term *teamwork* has become so overused and cliché that it's lost its true meaning.

Teamwork *does* make you better. But not in the way that you may think. And you can't have what Patrick Lencioni calls *artificial harmony* in his book, *The Five Dysfunctions of a Team.*

Ditch the Artificial Harmony

Picture this: A group of Navy SEALs dropped behind enemy lines in the dead of night. The mission? They have to rescue some high-ranking military hostages being held by a terrorist cell within a well-guarded compound. During the flight, the SEAL team decides on the course of action that would give them the greatest odds of success. They perform a High-Altitude, Low-Opening (HALO) jump to remain undetected as they infiltrate hostile territory. They approach the compound from the south,

Harmony does not translate to success. It's code for "not getting shit done."

where the greatest vulnerability appears to be. They silently take out several guards in their approach to the inner buildings where the hostages are being held. Using night vision and the cover of darkness, they make their way to the stairwell that snakes through the building to the floor where the hostages are sitting, waiting to be rescued. As they move to enter the stairwell, a member of the SEAL team named Sherman hesitates.

"What's the problem, Sherman?" one of the SEALs whispers.

Sherman shrugs awkwardly. "I just think it would be better to use the fire escape on the outside of the building."

"But we agreed this was the most direct route," says another SEAL.

"I didn't exactly agree," says Sherman. He shuffles his feet. "I was thinking about it while we were planning the mission but didn't want to, you know, seem like I was being contrarian."

Death stares from the rest of the SEALs. "You should have said something before!" one member barks. "We already have the plan," says another. "Let's just keep going."

Sherman stands his ground. "I don't think it's smart, guys. The fire escape seems much safer to get the hostages out."

"We don't have time for this sh—"

Pop! Pop! Pop! Pop! Pop! Five shots from a nearby guard who heard all the bickering, and it's game over. The SEALs are screwed. And so are the hostages.

If you think this is an absolutely ridiculous scenario, you are correct. I have the utmost respect for our US military, especially the Navy SEALs. I only used this far-fetched anecdote to illustrate the point that there is no way such elite operatives like the Navy SEALs would ever find themselves fighting about the best course of action while on the battlefield. They would have kicked ass, rescued the hostages, and been home in time for happy hour.

Leadership and teamwork in business can hardly be equated to the operations that America's finest willingly engage in to protect our freedom. But there is an important lesson here: artificial harmony is bullshit. There is no place for it, not on the battlefield and not in the boardroom.

Artificial harmony is a common phenomenon in many businesses, where employees avoid conflict to maintain a false sense of peace and unity. This often occurs when team members do not feel comfortable expressing their concerns or when there is a culture of fear.

To avoid artificial harmony, it's important to foster a culture of open communication.

To avoid artificial harmony, it's important to foster a culture of open communication and encourage *all* team members to express their opinions and concerns. This is done by implementing practices such as anonymous surveys, team-building exercises, and regular meetings where team members are encouraged to bring up concerns and ideas.

As a leader, you need to ensure that every employee has an equal opportunity to speak up during team meetings and that their opinions are valued. By avoiding artificial harmony, businesses can promote innovation, better decision-making, and a more productive work environment. This can lead to increased employee satisfaction, better customer service, and improved bottom-line results.

Make sure to prioritize open communication, and create a trust-based culture that values diverse perspectives. The results will speak for themselves.

I touched on this in an earlier chapter, but it bears repeating. In my company, when teams come out of a boardroom with a decision, everyone is ready to roll, giving no less than 100 percent. Not everyone may agree, but it was their responsibility to air any grievances, ask any questions, and challenge any decision among their colleagues. There are no impromptu meetings after meetings in the hallway with a select few for fear of offending anyone.

Part of teamwork making you better is providing a safe place to have healthy conversation in an environment where people can contest and question without offending or being offended. Nodding and agreeing is artificial harmony, and that may not be as deadly as in the aforementioned example, but it's devastating for the business. A true collaborative environment empowers everyone to be able to speak their mind, question one another, argue, sweat, and be pissed off. But it is in that healthy and respectful dialogue that you get to the best possible decision or plan.

Business is serious business. It's not for the faint of heart. And as enjoyable of an experience as it can and should be, the main goal of business is revenue and growth, not to provide an environment to find your BFF.

OK, maybe that's a bit harsh. But friendship at work is by no means a requirement for productivity. If you want warm and fuzzy, buy a gerbil. If you want to be successful in business, buy into the process of working as a team.

> **If you want warm and fuzzy, buy a gerbil. If you want to be successful in business, buy into the process of working as a team.**

Unless it's a family-owned business, you don't need a work "family." You already have friends and family beyond work. You're not there to make friends. Though I'll be the first to say that lasting friendships can certainly emerge from your workplace. Grinding it out side by side for years in a professional environment can definitely foster the kind of trust and respect that close friendships are based upon.

There are members of my team I've grown close enough to that I'd do just about anything for. But those relationships took time to develop. Just because we all wear the same logo on our hats doesn't mean I'll carry your couch up three flights of stairs.

Friendships are a by-product of success in business, not a requirement for success. Businesses ultimately fill a gap for customers and solve a problem. Teamwork means working together to solve that problem.

But beware of Band-Aids. Temporary solutions never lead to long-term success or scalability.

Never Solve Problems Temporarily

Earlier in the book, I described my great dismay at being chewed out by an unhappy customer for our "broken business model" as I was on my way to celebrate a recent success. No business owner wants an unhappy customer. Even one is too many. Yet when the same problem continues to arise again and again, you'll eventually wind up with a lot more than unhappy customers. You'll be out of business.

In this particular case, the unhappy customer was an insurance carrier who had just been chewed out by *their* customer, a policyholder who had been without air conditioning for ten days. When our team went to the policyholder's home to inspect the AC unit, they thought we were there to fix it, not to inspect, diagnose, and write up a report for the insurance company. Our client was under the same impression that we were there to repair the unit.

We obviously had a communication problem. And when other issues just like it kept cropping up, we realized fixing the problem on a case-by-case basis wasn't an effective strategy. We may have solved *a* problem, but we still hadn't solved *the* problem. Band-Aids only work for so long, and then they get soggy and fall off. And at the end of the day, we needed to figure out how to stop getting cut in the first place.

So we had a series of meetings, taking an objective, systematic approach to solving this problem for good. It sounds easier than it actually was, because we service nearly twelve thousand policyholders each month at the time of this writing. Putting in place a process to remind our client's client in twelve different ways that we are not there to repair, but to provide an expert, objective evaluation that saves insurance carriers and policyholders lots of time and work, was no easy task. But we eventually built it into our model and also started onboarding all new customers with special attention drawn to this issue.

Sure, it's tempting to focus solely on immediate concerns or short-term fixes. But taking a more long-term approach to problem-solving can help to establish a solid foundation for sustained growth and prosperity. It helps to foster a culture of innovation and creativity within an organization. When problems are viewed as opportunities for growth and improvement, employees are encouraged to think outside the box and come up with innovative solutions. This can lead to the development of new products or services, improved processes, and greater efficiency, which can contribute to increased competitiveness and profitability.

When problems are viewed as opportunities, employees are encouraged to think outside the box.

Permanently solving problems also helps to build customer loyalty and trust. When customers see that a business is committed to addressing and resolving issues in a timely and effective manner, they are more likely to continue doing business with that company. This can result in increased customer retention, word-of-mouth referrals, and a stronger reputation in the marketplace.

And let's not forget that solving problems for good also leads to cost savings over time. By addressing the root causes of issues rather than simply treating the symptoms, businesses can avoid repeated or ongoing expenses associated with temporary fixes. This can include things like equipment repairs, overtime pay for employees working to resolve the same issue repeatedly, or the cost of rework or product recalls.

No leader can build the perfect business model of success and exponential growth. There will undoubtedly be problems that pop up as the company changes through the years, through the evolving marketplace conditions, through the black swan events that are inevitable. But permanently solving problems is critical for achieving long-term success. By fostering a culture of dedication to process improvement, building customer trust, realizing cost savings, and creating a positive work environment, businesses can set themselves up for sustained growth and prosperity in the years to come.

Which leads to the most important aspect of teamwork: the common goal.

Working toward the Common Goal

No chapter about teamwork would be complete without acknowledging General Stanley McChrystal, the retired four-star general who served in the US Army for over three decades. He is widely regarded as one of the most accomplished and influential military leaders of his generation and is best known for his role in leading the Joint Special Operations Command (JSOC), a highly secretive and elite military unit, during the Iraq War.

McChrystal was known as a visionary military leader who challenged traditional assumptions about leadership and organizational structure. To this end, in 2015, he published his first bestseller, *Team of Teams: New Rules of Engagement for a Complex World*, which takes the strategies he leveraged in Iraq and applies them to business.

The book argues that traditional military structures, which are designed for hierarchical command and control, are not well-suited to the challenges of modern warfare. Instead, McChrystal advocates for a more decentralized and networked approach, where small teams work together in a dynamic and flexible manner to achieve their goals. Where did he get the idea? This is how terrorist cells work. It's what makes them effective and efficient. By watching what the enemy was doing, he learned how to defeat them at their own game.

To succeed, companies need to be able to respond quickly to changing market conditions.

And by empowering small teams to operate independently, businesses set themselves up for enduring success. The traditional command-and-control management style is outdated. To succeed in today's fast-paced and complex business environment, companies need to be agile, adaptable, and able to respond quickly to changing market conditions. As McChrystal contends, decentralized decision-making can make all the difference. In the military context, this means empowering small teams to make decisions based on the information available to them rather than relying on a top-down command structure.

In the business world, this could mean giving employees more autonomy to make decisions and encouraging collaboration between teams. By breaking down silos and encouraging cross-functional collaboration, businesses can become more agile and better able to respond to changing market conditions. This also means regular check-ins between leaders and teams and a focus on transparency and open communication—regular meetings between managers and employees to discuss progress and challenges as well as a culture of open communication and feedback.

When individuals excel, the team excels. When the team excels, the department excels. When the department excels, the company goals are realized. In most companies, the common goal is tied to revenue. For example, once we decide on our revenue goal for the year, we break that down into smaller goals that each team and each department is responsible for. We will instantly know if we're off track based on real-time data on our scoreboard. And we know which individual or team is struggling to hit their targets.

> **When individuals excel, the team excels. When the team excels, the department excels. When the department excels, the company goals are realized.**

In 2021, we hit our company goal at 11:30 a.m. on December 31. We may have used nearly every minute of the year, but we made it. Even after our first private equity transaction years ago, we stayed up until 11:59 p.m. on the last day of the first quarter end to make sure we hit the goal we had set. There were no extra bonuses or partner distributions to be made if we did. But watching the company goal had become so engrained in the leadership, in who we are, we just couldn't help ourselves.

When team goals are that deeply embedded, you've created a true team. That kind of teamwork is what drives success, decides outcomes, and ensures legacy.

A Fairy Tale about Teamwork

Once upon a time, in a far-off kingdom, a group of workers was tasked with building a grand cathedral in their village. The team was made up of skilled craftsmen, architects, and laborers, and they all took great pride in their work. The project was massive, and the team worked tirelessly for years, overcoming many obstacles along the way.

As the project neared completion, tensions began to rise among the team members. One new member in particular, an apprentice stonemason named Willy, was constantly being ignored. Over time he became jealous of all the praise being rained down on the senior craftsmen and began to secretly undermine their work. He would thin out the mortar, wet the wooden framework so it would swell, and replace the architects' measurements with the incorrect numbers. These actions started to cause tension in the team, and the project suffered as a result. The workers stopped communicating effectively, began pointing fingers, and ultimately stopped trusting one another.

As the cathedral was finally completed, the team members stood together, looking at their magnificent creation. The joy of the moment made them forget the tension, and they all embraced, apologized, and rejoiced together. They even apologized to Willy for not taking his feelings into consideration and gave him an award for his apprenticeship. Willy was moved to tears. But it was too fucking late. The cathedral was riddled with flaws, and it collapsed just minutes after its completion, crushing everyone, including Willy.

The village was devastated. Rumors began to circulate about how the workers' lack of collaboration had led to a tragic and irreversible outcome. A month later, the pile of rubble that was once a glorious cathedral was bulldozed away, and a Dollar Tree store was erected in its place.

Years passed, and the story of the grand cathedral became a legend in the kingdom. People would visit the Dollar Tree store where the cathedral once stood, and they would remember the tragedy that occurred beneath their feet as they munched on knock-off Gummi Bears. They realized that petty disputes and lack of collaboration can have catastrophic consequences. The tragedy of the cathedral remained a stark reminder of their mistakes, and they never forgot the importance of working together as a team to achieve a common goal.

Reflections Make You Better

Teamwork in business is essential as it enables individuals to pool their diverse talents and resources to achieve a common goal. Collaboration among team members encourages creativity, innovation, and better decision-making. By working together, team members can support and motivate one another, leading to higher job satisfaction and productivity. Teamwork promotes effective communication and a sense of accountability, ensuring that each team member is responsible for their assigned tasks and contributes to the team's success. In today's competitive business world, teamwork has become an indispensable aspect of achieving success and staying ahead of the curve. Here are a few tips on why teamwork in business is critical:

- **Diverse Skills and Expertise:** Each member of a team brings different skills, knowledge, and experience to the table. By working together, the team can combine their diverse strengths to accomplish goals and solve problems that would be impossible to achieve alone. Differing opinions are critical as well. If everyone on the team has the same opinion on a topic, it's time to get nervous.
- **Improved Communication:** Working in a team allows for open communication, where ideas can be shared, and feedback can be given in a safe and constructive environment. This results in better decision-making and a more efficient work process.

- **Increased Creativity:** When working in a team, members can bounce ideas off one another, sparking creativity and innovation. This can lead to new ideas and solutions that would not have been possible without collaboration.
- **Higher Motivation and Accountability:** Teamwork encourages members to support and motivate one another, leading to higher job satisfaction and productivity. In addition, working in a team creates a sense of accountability, as each member is responsible for their assigned tasks and contributing to the team's success.
- **More Efficient Use of Resources:** By working together, a team can share resources and distribute tasks, resulting in a more efficient use of time and money, allowing you to invest in taking your resources to the next level.

ELIEVE IN BETTER / THE EVOLUTION OF CORE PRINCIPLES
HAT PIONEERED AN INDUSTRY // AUTHENTICITY MAKES
OU BETTER // BELIEVE IN BETTER / THE EVOLUTION
F CORE PRINCIPLES THAT PIONEERED AN INDUSTRY //
USTLING MAKES YOU BETTER // BELIEVE IN BETTER /
HE EVOLUTION OF CORE PRINCIPLES THAT PIONEERED AN
NDUSTRY // BELIEVE IN BETTER / THE EVOLUTION OF CORE
RINCIPLES THAT PIONEERED AN INDUSTRY // SELLING
AKES YOU BETTER // BELIEVE IN BETTER / THE EVOLUTION
F CORE PRINCIPLES THAT PIONEERED AN INDUSTRY //
ELIEVE IN BETTER / THE EVOLUTION OF CORE PRINCIPLES
HAT PIONEERED AN INDUSTRY // BELIEVE IN BETTER /
HE EVOLUTION OF CORE PRINCIPLES THAT PIONEERED AN
NDUSTRY // BELIEVE IN BETTER / THE EVOLUTION OF CORE
RINCIPLES THAT PIONEERED AN INDUSTRY // UNDERSTANDING
ERSPECTIVE MAKES YOU BETTER //BELIEVE IN BETTER /
HE EVOLUTION OF CORE PRINCIPLES THAT PIONEERED AN
NDUSTRY // BELIEVE IN BETTER / THE EVOLUTION OF CORE
RINCIPLES THAT PIONEERED AN INDUSTRY // TEAMWORK
AKES YOU BETTER // BELIEVE IN BETTER / THE EVOLUTION
F CORE PRINCIPLES THAT PIONEERED AN INDUSTRY //
AKING ACTION MAKES YOU BETTER // BELIEVE IN BETTER
 THE EVOLUTION OF CORE PRINCIPLES THAT PIONEERED AN
NDUSTRY // TRANSPARENCY MAKES YOU BETTER // BELIEVE
N BETTER / THE EVOLUTION OF CORE PRINCIPLES THAT
IONEERED AN INDUSTRY // DRIVING PROFITABILITY MAKES
OU BETTER // THE EVOLUTION OF CORE PRINCIPLES THAT
IONEERED AN INDUSTRY // PROCESS MAKES YOU BETTER //
ELIEVE IN BETTER / THE EVOLUTION OF CORE PRINCIPLES
HAT PIONEERED AN INDUSTRY // CHANGE MAKES YOU BETTER
/ BELIEVE IN BETTER / THE EVOLUTION OF CORE PRINCIPLE

BELIEVE IN BETTER / THE EVOLUTION OF CORE PRINCIPLE
THAT PIONEERED AN INDUSTRY // AUTHENTICITY MAKE
YOU BETTER // BELIEVE IN BETTER / THE EVOLUTIO
OF CORE PRINCIPLES THAT PIONEERED AN INDUSTRY /
HUSTLING MAKES YOU BETTER // BELIEVE IN BETTER
THE EVOLUTION OF CORE PRINCIPLES THAT PIONEERED A
INDUSTRY // BELIEVE IN BETTER / THE EVOLUTION OF COR
PRINCIPLES THAT PIONEERED AN INDUSTRY // SELLIN
MAKES YOU BETTER // BELIEVE IN BETTER / THE EVOLUTIO
OF CORE PRINCIPLES THAT PIONEERED AN INDUSTRY /
BELIEVE IN BETTER / THE EVOLUTION OF CORE PRINCIPLE
THAT PIONEERED AN INDUSTRY // BELIEVE IN BETTER
THE EVOLUTION OF CORE PRINCIPLES THAT PIONEERED A
INDUSTRY // BELIEVE IN BETTER / THE EVOLUTION OF COR
PRINCIPLES THAT PIONEERED AN INDUSTRY // UNDERSTANDIN
PERSPECTIVE MAKES YOU BETTER //BELIEVE IN BETTER
THE EVOLUTION OF CORE PRINCIPLES THAT PIONEERED A
INDUSTRY // BELIEVE IN BETTER / THE EVOLUTION OF COR
PRINCIPLES THAT PIONEERED AN INDUSTRY // TEAMWOR
MAKES YOU BETTER // BELIEVE IN BETTER / THE EVOLUTIO
OF CORE PRINCIPLES THAT PIONEERED AN INDUSTRY /
TAKING ACTION MAKES YOU BETTER // BELIEVE IN BETTE
/ THE EVOLUTION OF CORE PRINCIPLES THAT PIONEERED A
INDUSTRY // TRANSPARENCY MAKES YOU BETTER // BELIEV
IN BETTER / THE EVOLUTION OF CORE PRINCIPLES THA
PIONEERED AN INDUSTRY // DRIVING PROFITABILITY MAKE
YOU BETTER // THE EVOLUTION OF CORE PRINCIPLES THA
PIONEERED AN INDUSTRY // PROCESS MAKES YOU BETTER /
BELIEVE IN BETTER / THE EVOLUTION OF CORE PRINCIPLE
THAT PIONEERED AN INDUSTRY // CHANGE MAKES YOU BETTE
// BELIEVE IN BETTER / THE EVOLUTION OF CORE PRINCIPL

Taking Action
Makes You Better

Well done is better than well said.

—BENJAMIN FRANKLIN

Years ago, we hired an executive for our team from the insurance industry. Stellar guy, outstanding skills, just a perfect fit for our company. Before long we ended up hopping a flight together for a meeting out of state. If you don't remember what I'm like when I'm flying, I suggest you re-read the chapter on how Hustling Makes You Better. Needless to say, as soon as my new executive pulled out his laptop and turned on an in-flight movie, I lost my mind.

"What the fuck are you doing?" I asked pleasantly.

"Watching a movie," he replied. "Why?"

"Because we may be forty thousand feet in the air, but it's still a Tuesday afternoon. Let's make the most of it."

In his defense, he didn't do anything any different from the millions of executives who jet all over the world. And I share this story with a little humor and a lot of respect for this man. But taking action—at all times—is all I know. Period.

To balance this triangle of taking action, you need to balance time, productivity, and cost. At *all* times.

As a leader, and more importantly as an entrepreneur, there is an equilateral triangle around the words *taking action*. One of the triangle segments represents *time*. Another represents *productivity*. And the final segment represents *cost*. To balance this triangle of taking action, you need to balance time, productivity, and cost. Not sometimes. Not most of the time. At *all* times.

When I decide to take action and fly to another state, or even another country, there are all kinds of expenses involved—flight, hotel, ground transportation, meals, and so forth. And the hours or days eaten up as opposed to having a Zoom call can be astronomical. So, from my perspective, the productivity of taking the action of flying better be proportional to the cost and time.

That means every minute counts. Sure, maybe the meeting will result in a huge sale. But maybe it won't. By filling all available time with productive action, even if the trip is a bust, work still got done. Now I'm not saying that catching a nap on a plane is a waste of time. It may be necessary to prepare and refresh for whatever lies ahead. But movies? Facebook? Crocheting? Not on my watch. Now, have I ever been accused of taking a day trip to Boston with a key executive team leader, just to have two hours of dedicated collaboration time each way and enjoy a cup of clam chowder? Sure. Did we need to pay for the flight and the chowder to get four hours of dedicated time on the topic? No. But it worked.

Flying provides one of the rare opportunities to unplug (sort of) and be free of most distractions. I actually get excited to work in the air. Sometimes it's catching up on the to-do list while it's quiet. Other times I like to just sit and focus on the meetings to come.

I don't even remember traveling during the first five years of my company without a serious sense of urgency to get operational reports written and approved while I was on the plane. Then when I landed, or if I was sitting in the parking lot waiting to go into the meeting, I was on my laptop trying to finish. Some might say, "You should have invested in more people." But as a business, we weren't there yet. The entrepreneurs reading this know exactly what I mean. Back then, it was just me and a few other people, and we had to do it all. Sure, I could have watched endless episodes of *Mad Men; Cheers; Mary Tyler Moore; Caddy Shack; Glengarry Glenn Ross; Boiler Room; Wall Street; Thank You for Smoking; Snatch; Lock, Stock, and Two Smoking Barrels; Anchorman; The Ladies Man; Saturday Night Live; Seinfeld; PJ 20; Sonic Highways; Fletch!; Almost Famous; Moneyball; Nirvana Live at Reading; Audioslave Live in Cuba*; any Leo DiCaprio movie; *Ted; Stepbrothers; Tropic Thunder; Wedding Crashers; 8 Mile; Tommy*

Boy; Planes, Trains, and Automobiles; or *Miller's Crossing* on my laptop instead, but I guarantee you that you wouldn't be reading this book right now had I dialed it in.

That's why I just can't believe my eyes when I see the executives around me watching movies or playing Candy Crush. I think about how much company time and money they are wasting. Traveling doesn't mean working. They aren't really taking action. They're just acting like they are acting.

Which really isn't acting at all.

Acting versus Acting like Acting

When I get home from traveling or after a super long day at the office, all I can think about is crashing. But suddenly my two babies, daughter and son, are reaching for a hug, wanting to spend time with their Daddy. I could easily act like I'm taking action; dial it in and sit with my phone on my lap watching TikTok videos while she colors. But what message does that send? What does that say about my investment in her? I'd rather push a little harder and get on the floor with her to play with some blocks, or paint, or color than pretend like I'm engaged.

Imitating action isn't really action, so don't fool yourself. Acting productive may seem like a good strategy to check things off a list, but it's not a recipe for long-term success, especially in business. Taking action is about getting things done by making meaningful contributions. Like Dale Carnagie said, "Do the hard jobs first. The easy jobs will take care of themselves." Acting like acting just leads to a lack of progress, a whole lot of missed opportunities, and a loss of trust and respect from colleagues and superiors.

I've seen my share of employees—and worse, high-paid leaders—who sit at a desk all day playing office. Instead of being productive, they are spending their next distribution or commission check, surfing LinkedIn or other social media, getting caught up on their personal emails, or maybe calling their country club for an itemized receipt of the last bar tab. My advice for these folks: For the love of God, please check in with your spouse, please take care of anything urgent with the kids, but stop *fucking off* on company time and do the real work! Eventually the whole team suffers, not to mention the company, because they end up missing deadlines, producing subpar work, or creating a negative work environment for their teams because they are leading with a bad example.

Outside of the blatant employees who fake being busy is another category of nonproductivity—hamsters. These are the employees who spend their time on the wheel of tasks that aren't actually important or necessary. They may spend hours on a task that could be done in minutes or focus on tasks that don't align with the company's goals or pri-

> **Leaders need to make sure *all* employees have a clear understanding of their responsibilities and the company's goals and priorities.**

orities. While they may appear productive, their lack of focus and direction can lead to wasted time and resources and may even harm the company's bottom line.

Sometimes, they may not have a clear understanding of their responsibilities or the company's goals and priorities. Other times, they may be overwhelmed by their workload and unsure of where to focus their time and energy. Sometimes, they just might be unmotivated or disengaged, not fully invested in the performance of the company.

Regardless of the reason, the result is the same: a lack of productivity and progress toward the company's goals. This can be especially damaging if the employee is in a leadership position because their lack of focus and direction can have a ripple effect on their team and the company as a whole. Trust me, I get it. Holding yourself accountable to commitments isn't always easy. But it's necessary.

To avoid this situation, leaders need to make sure *all* employees have a clear understanding of their responsibilities and the company's goals and priorities. This can be achieved through aligned KPIs, metrics, and transparency in performance and data, as well as communication with managers and colleagues. And let's not forget ongoing training and professional development. By staying informed and engaged, employees can ensure that they're focusing their time and energy on tasks that are truly important and necessary and contributing to the success of the company.

However, employees who are truly productive are those who focus on achieving their goals and delivering results. They prioritize their tasks, manage their time effectively, and stay focused on their objectives. They may not always look busy, but they consistently deliver high-quality work and contribute to the success of their team and the company as a whole.

Ultimately, taking action makes you better because it drives more action. If next steps do not develop and result in taking further action, then it's not the right action.

Although, sometimes, any action is better than no action at all.

Nothing Is Worse Than No Action

Back in the day, we had zero structure to our marketing efforts. Like many growing businesses, we were so caught up in operations that we really didn't focus on marketing until we needed more leads to drive more revenue. So we'd react in the moment—push out a press release, an email blast, or a blog post.

Was there some sort of well-developed strategy involved? Not really. Could we have taken more time to build out content for a marketing funnel and create a comprehensive campaign? Sure, but at what cost? Remember the "taking action" triangle? We didn't have time to waste, nor could we afford to. That meant being productive was our only option.

But beyond generating leads, taking action also provided another valuable asset: experience. One of the most significant benefits of taking action in business is the experience that comes with it. When a company makes a decision or initiates a project, it gains valuable insights into the market, the competition, and its own capabilities. This knowledge can then be used to refine business strategies and make better-informed decisions moving forward. Even if a particular action does not result in the outcome you had hoped for, the experience itself can be a valuable source of lessons that contribute to the long-term success of the organization.

Creating a culture of taking action also fosters tangible process improvement, innovation, and adaptability within a company. When a business is proactive and decisive, it encourages employees to think creatively and develop new ideas. This mindset can lead to the discovery of new products, services, or strategies that can give a company a competitive edge in the market. A willingness to take action will also help a business adapt quickly to changing circumstances, enabling it to seize opportunities and stay ahead of competitors.

Inaction creates a negative feedback loop, where a lack of progress leads to lower morale and decreased productivity. But when a company takes action, it generates a positive cycle of achievement and motivation. Employees feel a sense of accomplishment and purpose, which, in turn, inspires them to work harder.

Taking action also signals confidence to stakeholders like investors, customers, and partners. When a business demonstrates the ability to make decisions and pursue its goals assertively, it projects an image of stability and trustworthiness. This simple operating principle of "doing what you say you are going to do" by taking action creates a perception, a reputation that can help attract new customers, secure funding, and foster stronger relationships.

When a business demonstrates the ability to make decisions and pursue its goals assertively, it projects an image of stability and trustworthiness.

Putting out a press release on the fly or shooting out a last-minute email blast might not have been the most effective or efficient action, but by doing nothing, we were guaranteeing a 100 percent failure rate for leads. We had at least increased our odds. Not taking action means relying on luck, and luck never built a successful business. No, not even casinos.

Speaking of odds and casinos, there is a direct relationship between risk and taking action.

The Relationship of Risk and Action

I've made massive mistakes and wasted ridiculous amounts of resources hiring the wrong people. All kinds of time, money, and productivity out the window because I didn't properly weigh the risk of the decision. But early on in business, that's what happens—you make the easy decision when filling a position. And sometimes it turns out to be the wrong person.

And then there are other times that the risk pays off, like back in 2016 when we looked to take our company to market and find the best financial partner and value for our company. By making this decision, everything we created and built over the years was on the line.

In the weeks prior, one of our partners had a random encounter with a major private equity group on, of all places, the putting green of his country club. Within a week (and a few conversations plus a financial summary later), they made a valuation of roughly $50 million for our company. Yes, just like that. They were hoping to preempt any sort of process that would include getting us on the market. Internally, we had estimated our valuation to be around $30 million, so you can only imagine how excited we were to have it nearly doubled.

My partner at the time kept pushing us to sell, but the plan we all committed to was to take the time to hire an investment banker to go through the valuation process, which takes an incredible amount of time and energy with a big risk of taking your eye off whatever has created your success as a business. It was a huge decision, and the risk was high, so I wanted time to do our due diligence. I was dedicated to doing the hard work and running a thorough investment banking sell-side process to find the best private equity group for us at the time. We interviewed multiple investment bankers over multiple meetings for each and made a clear decision and hired the very best. Picture Ari Gold (*Entourage*), Charlize Theron (*Mad Max*), George Clooney (*Oceans 11*), and Mel Gibson (*Braveheart*) flying in on a pack of those black Sikorsky S-76 helicopters from *Succession* to represent your business players.

So the investment banker we had hired went out to 150 private equity groups, and somewhere around 80 of them submitted indications of interest. Fourteen of those companies ended up attending an all-day management presentation and dinner.

During this long process, my former partner kept complaining about the time and effort we were wasting in even hiring an investment banker, until we got an offer for $80-plus million. I was

As the potential risks to the business increase, taking the time necessary to carefully assess the situation and make informed choices is imperative.

dedicated to finishing what we started. This was a deliberate plan we set, and we were going to fucking finish it. Revisionist history here? Nope. By doing the hard work and finishing, we sold for 65 percent greater value.

When we're evaluating an action to take at Alpine Intel, we like to rely on the 80/20 rule. If the action to be taken has an 80 percent probability of success or higher, we do it. But only if the risk involved is moderate. High-risk decisions, like in the valuation example, are another matter entirely.

Recently, we were working through taking action on a $200 million acquisition. Talk about high risk. For that kind of decision, we need to be 90–95 percent confident. There's not a lot of wiggle room for error at that level. Going back to our triangle, we need to stretch out the segment of time based on the risk level. The higher the risk, the longer that side of the triangle needs to be.

Sure, taking action is better than remaining stagnant. But it is equally important to properly weigh the risks involved in each decision. As the potential risks to the business increase, taking the time necessary to carefully assess the situation and make informed choices is imperative.

One of the most important aspects of weighing risk in decision-making is conducting thorough research and analysis that remains focused on the customer's perspective—the perspective of who is paying the bills. Because without revenue, the business is nothing—revenue is Queen! Gathering comprehensive information about the market, competition, and potential outcomes can help leaders make more accurate predictions and better understand the potential consequences of their actions. Also doing some scenario planning and considering various possible outcomes can provide valuable insights into the potential risks and benefits of different courses of action. By taking the time to analyze the available data and consider all possible scenarios that drive top-line revenue, companies can make more informed decisions and minimize potential risks.

Properly weighing risk when considering particular actions also means evaluating the company's capacity to absorb potential losses or setbacks. As a leader, you should consider your company's financial stability, organizational structure, and overall resilience before embarking on a high-risk venture. It's so easy to get caught up in excitement and momentum that are created by those close to your business, those who get paid commissions and fees to add risk to your business—risk that, as soon as the decision is final, is *your* responsibility to mitigate risk, grow, and manage. If the potential negative consequences of a decision outweigh the company's ability to recover, it may be wise to seek alternative solutions or take more time to assess the situation. The process of introspection can help a business make better decisions that balance growth and innovation with stability and security.

Striking a healthy balance between risk-taking and risk aversion can be tricky. Oftentimes it involves considering the potential opportunity cost of *inaction*. For instance, you may need to weigh the potential gains from jumping on an opportunity against the potential losses if you decide to wait.

Like with the investment banker, you can definitely benefit from consulting with experts on high-risk decisions and take advantage of their reach into whatever their particular expertise is as well as their relationships. Professionals can provide valuable insights, alternative viewpoints, and specialized knowledge that can help a company make more informed choices. By leveraging the expertise of others, businesses can better evaluate the risks involved in their decisions and potentially identify opportunities they might have otherwise overlooked.

With high-risk actions, business leaders need to reserve the right to take all the time necessary. You can't rush a decision that could be potentially dangerous to your business. If you were out in the woods and had a bear charging you, would you rather have a shotgun that will scatter wide and probably hit the bear but have little impact or a high-powered sniper rifle and take a little time to make that perfect kill shot?

(Note to reader: no animals were harmed in the writing of this chapter.)

A Fairy Tale about Taking Action

Once upon a time, there were two business partners named Alice and Bob. Alice was a hardworking person, always taking action and looking for ways to improve the business, while Bob was lazy and often tried to look important without doing much work.

Alice and Bob had built a successful company together, but Alice was growing increasingly frustrated with Bob's lack of contribution. While Alice worked tirelessly to grow the business, Bob spent most of his time taking long lunches and attending meetings just to look busy.

One day, Alice proposed a new idea for a product line that she believed would bring in significant revenue. Bob agreed that it was a good idea but didn't offer to help with any of the work required to make it happen. Alice was left to do all the research, development, and marketing on her own.

As the launch date approached, Alice grew tired and stressed from doing all the work alone. Bob continued to act as if he were the brains behind the operation, even though he had done nothing to contribute. When the product launched, it was a huge success, and the company experienced a surge in revenue. Bob tried to take credit for the success, but Alice was fed up and decided to confront him about his lack of contribution.

Bob tried to defend himself, saying that he had other important responsibilities to attend to, but Alice was not convinced. She realized that Bob was just trying to look important without actually doing anything, and it was damaging their partnership and the company's success. Alice and Bob parted ways. A few weeks later, Bob realized how much he had taken his partnership with Alice for granted. He knew he had made a mistake by not contributing his fair share to the business, and he wanted to make things right.

Bob reached out to Alice and apologized for his laziness and selfish behavior. He explained that his ego had gotten in the way. He was determined to turn things around and be a better partner. But it was too fucking late.

Alice had found a new partner, Martin, an ex-MMA fighter who kicked Bob's ass, breaking 97 percent of Bob's bones. As he lay there in the grass looking up at vultures circling, Bob finally understood the repercussions of not taking action.

Alice and Martin went on to have tremendous success with their business, eventually going public in 2023.

Reflections Make You Better

Taking action is crucial in business because it's what separates successful companies from those that fail. While planning and strategy are important, they're useless without execution. Business owners need to be proactive, take calculated risks, and adapt to change if they want to stay ahead of the competition. Here are some tips for taking action in business:

- **Prioritize Tasks and Do the Hard Work First:** The hard problem to solve, the complex, the thing on your list that pains you to work on. That's the most important. It's easy to get bogged down with an overwhelming to-do list, but prioritizing tasks can help you stay focused on what really matters. Consider which tasks will have the biggest impact on your business goals, and tackle those first. This will help you make the most of your time and energy.

- **Break Down Larger Goals into Smaller, Achievable Tasks to Make Them More Manageable:** Big goals can seem daunting and overwhelming, but breaking them down into smaller, achievable tasks can help you make progress and stay motivated. Identify the steps you need to take to achieve your larger goal, and focus on completing those one by one.

- **Be Open to Feedback and Willing to Make Changes When Necessary:** Feedback is a valuable tool for improving your business. Listen to your customers, employees, and colleagues, and be open to their suggestions. Don't be afraid to make changes to your business model or strategy if you see an opportunity for improvement.

- **Set Deadlines and Hold Yourself Accountable for Meeting Them:** Deadlines can help you stay on track and ensure that you're making progress toward your goals. Set realistic deadlines for yourself, and hold yourself accountable for meeting them. This will help you stay motivated and focused on the tasks at hand.

- **Surround Yourself with a Supportive Team:** Running a business can be overwhelming, but you don't have to do it alone. Surround yourself with a supportive team with aligned incentives, and adopt an ethos of building frameworks that allow you to delegate and hold your team accountable. Adopt a standard of delegating, and trust your team to execute, so you can spend your time on the things that no one else *can do*.

- **Continuously Educate Yourself on Industry Trends and Best Practices to Stay Ahead of the Game:** Continuously educate yourself on the macro information that influences the trends in your industry. The business, regulatory, and political worlds are constantly evolving, and with these changes come opportunity and risk.

BELIEVE IN BETTER / THE EVOLUTION OF CORE PRINCIPLES THAT PIONEERED AN INDUSTRY // AUTHENTICITY MAKES YOU BETTER // BELIEVE IN BETTER / THE EVOLUTION OF CORE PRINCIPLES THAT PIONEERED AN INDUSTRY // HUSTLING MAKES YOU BETTER // BELIEVE IN BETTER / THE EVOLUTION OF CORE PRINCIPLES THAT PIONEERED AN INDUSTRY // BELIEVE IN BETTER / THE EVOLUTION OF CORE PRINCIPLES THAT PIONEERED AN INDUSTRY // SELLING MAKES YOU BETTER // BELIEVE IN BETTER / THE EVOLUTION OF CORE PRINCIPLES THAT PIONEERED AN INDUSTRY // BELIEVE IN BETTER / THE EVOLUTION OF CORE PRINCIPLES THAT PIONEERED AN INDUSTRY // BELIEVE IN BETTER / THE EVOLUTION OF CORE PRINCIPLES THAT PIONEERED AN INDUSTRY // BELIEVE IN BETTER / THE EVOLUTION OF CORE PRINCIPLES THAT PIONEERED AN INDUSTRY // UNDERSTANDING PERSPECTIVE MAKES YOU BETTER //BELIEVE IN BETTER / THE EVOLUTION OF CORE PRINCIPLES THAT PIONEERED AN INDUSTRY // BELIEVE IN BETTER / THE EVOLUTION OF CORE PRINCIPLES THAT PIONEERED AN INDUSTRY // TEAMWORK MAKES YOU BETTER // BELIEVE IN BETTER / THE EVOLUTION OF CORE PRINCIPLES THAT PIONEERED AN INDUSTRY // TAKING ACTION MAKES YOU BETTER // BELIEVE IN BETTER / THE EVOLUTION OF CORE PRINCIPLES THAT PIONEERED AN INDUSTRY // **TRANSPARENCY MAKES YOU BETTER** // BELIEVE IN BETTER / THE EVOLUTION OF CORE PRINCIPLES THAT PIONEERED AN INDUSTRY // DRIVING PROFITABILITY MAKES YOU BETTER // THE EVOLUTION OF CORE PRINCIPLES THAT PIONEERED AN INDUSTRY // PROCESS MAKES YOU BETTER // BELIEVE IN BETTER / THE EVOLUTION OF CORE PRINCIPLES THAT PIONEERED AN INDUSTRY // CHANGE MAKES YOU BETTER // BELIEVE IN BETTER / THE EVOLUTION OF CORE PRINCIPLE

Transparency Makes You Better

Transparency is like a rare gem in the business world—everyone claims to have it, but few are willing to show you the real sparkle.

—UNKNOWN

Transparency—it's a buzzword we hear thrown around in the business world all the time. But what exactly is it?

Within the context of Alpine Intel, it's a competitive differentiator. It's a management tool, a scoreboard, a communication medium. Transparency means putting everything out there for all to see. It's about leaving no space for confusion, misunderstanding, or miscommunication. You expose your data, your performance metrics, your plans, and your challenges. This means there's no looking back, no secrecy, no posturing. You have your goals and the performance metrics right there on the scoreboard. No bullshit, just facts. And just think about all the productive hours you can get back by not having to ask questions like, "So how are we doing in this area? How is Thomas trending in his sales activity?"

Transparency doesn't end at work, either. It seeps into our personal lives as well. At least it should. We all know the guy who wants to go to the bar with a couple of buddies after work to celebrate St. Patrick's Day. It's best if he's totally transparent with his wife—let her know he'd like to drink a few Guinnesses for a couple of hours and then drop into an Uber and head back home. Irrespective of the fact that his wife and women like her are among the most patient humans in the world, this level of transparency gives her the confidence that he won't tell her one thing and do another. He could easily say he'll be working late and make up some lame excuse, but all that does is destroy her faith in him and ruin his good time. Sure, it's an uncomfortable conversation to have, but it's way better than the alternative. And once the initial sting is over, he can openly enjoy his time out and belly laugh without being eaten alive by guilt or the anxiety of getting caught.

This illustrates one of the remarkable things about transparency—the freedom it brings. Being transparent eliminates guilt and uncertainty, allowing us to focus on what truly matters. No more walking around with the weight of secrets or hidden agendas. By being open and honest, we can prioritize our actions and regain control of our time and energy.

Don't lead with a bad example by wasting precious company dollars on an industry conference just to go sit at a hotel bar for three days during the week. Be deliberate about taking a team-building overnight trip where you spend half of what you would at a conference, but stay at a five-star hotel, eating better food and scheduling a mandatory two-hour fitness or relaxation time for your leaders. Be deliberate and transparent about what you are doing. You will spend less and be much more productive, creating more value for your company in the future. It's about being honest and upfront, not just with others but also with yourself.

As a leader, you need to end the guilt trips and embrace transparency as a core value in your company. Set an example by being honest and forthcoming yourself. Create a culture of transparency where team members feel comfortable being honest and open. Foster an environment that values authenticity and encourages individuals to speak up without fear of judgment or repercussions. Live in the "trust tree" where people can say it here and now.

> **Leaders need to end the guilt trips and embrace transparency as a core value.**

But as with most things, easier said than done, right? Transparency is not all rainbows and unicorns. In fact, it even has a cost associated with it—a tax, you might say.

The Transparency Tax

If you've made it this far, you have probably guessed that my sense of humor is a little, well, warped. That's me being me, fully transparent. So in a chapter about transparency, it shouldn't surprise you when I reference an animated film from 2004 called *Team America: World Police*, which at the time I found hilarious. By today's standards, however, the movie is entirely politically incorrect and would never have been made.

Like many films of the era, it's a satirical comedy film that skillfully critiques political and cultural aspects of society. Within the movie is one of those ear worms that chew into your brain, a memorable song called "Freedom Isn't Free," which contains the following line: "Freedom ain't free, it costs a buck.09." This cleverly underscores the idea that freedom carries a price, a tax if you will.

Just like transparency. Speaking of which, did I willfully stretch on the correlation of the quote here just to have a *Team America* quote in my book? Absolutely.

We all face situations that require us to address uncomfortable truths. We might know someone who's brilliant socially but not fulfilling their professional duties. Addressing these issues is tough, but it's a tax we must pay to foster a productive and honest work environment. The thing is, transparency isn't just about honesty. It's a vital tax we pay for the smooth functioning of our teams and organizations. The cost of not being transparent always ends up higher, as it wastes energy, resources, and, most important, time.

Think of it this way: What happens when you fail to pay your corporate taxes? Penalties, audits, investigations. And that's if you are lucky. Believe me, it was incredibly painful to stroke a check for the 2016 tax season for double digits in the millions of dollars. But we had to do it. As a leader, you aren't simply flaunting an inflated cash balance, making you artificially feel good about the health of the company. You are living lean, in the transparent present. You're acknowledging the debts that require payment.

Transparency in leadership is not an option; it's a requirement across my companies. It's a beacon of communication, a guiding principle that leaves no room for ambiguity. When everyone on the team knows the score, the room for "I didn't know" is annihilated. A visible scoreboard eliminates excuses, promotes honesty, and reduces misunderstandings to a bare minimum.

Being transparent also means shedding the facade of an ideal day, confronting the growing guilt of unaddressed issues until they morph into even bigger problems. A lack of transparency can often lead to a point of no return—a failure or an avoidable loss.

Nothing rang truer than when I worked in tech sales. Some sales reps were incredibly talented at making waves through the management of the organization—selling their pipeline of demand generation through the power of their relationships and telling stories instead of answering the real questions at weekly sales pipeline drill downs. Dancing around direct sales-cycle milestones with talk of dark room steak and wine dinners with key decision-makers from accounts. Dodging transparency of what was going on with the true technical value sold to the system architects who would be using the technology every day. Or failing to do the hard work by getting the account to commit to a two-hour software demo that would truly judge their interest and decision-makers while documenting the problem we were solving.

Guess what? As previously stated, I'm unbullshitable and have a 0.1000 batting average on these kinds of topics. The year end came calling, and I specifically remember my peers thinking they were going to make $1.2 million in commission, based on their reputation and commitments made over a handful of massive opportunities. Instead, two days after the dust settled from year end, the leadership walked their hinies out of the building, and we all watched them get into their leased Maseratis and ride off into the sunset, back to their country club life in the burbs.

Transparency isn't always easy. It comes with its challenges. Being transparent means confronting hard truths, dealing with uncomfortable facts, and having difficult conversations. But the tax of being nontransparent is even higher. Without transparency, you're living in a world of delusions, letting problems build, and ultimately missing the mark.

Transparency is the secret sauce that builds trust, loyalty, and commitment within your company. With your team, clients, and stakeholders, transparency creates a strong foundation for lasting relationships. When you pay the transparency tax, you earn their trust and loyalty, making them more invested in your company's success.

But transparency isn't just about conveying information—it's about how you deliver it.

The Charisma of Transparency

When you think about it, transparency is a type of charisma. The bravery to face issues head-on, to discuss them openly, and to own the outcomes draws respect and trust from your customers and team. It's about more than capturing attention or leading—it's about fostering relationships built on honesty, empathy, and mutual respect.

The charisma of transparency is best demonstrated in what we call "the human touch." It's the tone of your voice, your body language, and the empathy you project when delivering a difficult message. Take, for instance, a situation where you need to tell a team member they are underperforming. Show them a bullet-pointed list of short-comings without warmth or compassion, and they're likely to show you their long finger. But a human-centered delivery, acknowledging the issues and outlining a clear path to resolution, can have a dramatic impact on the response. That's why it's critical to have transparency from the very beginning, creating goals that are aligned with the team member or direct report.

In the business world, the charisma of transparency is often exemplified by leaders who skillfully navigate complex situations with honesty and charm. You know, by saying something like Ed Harris's character said in *Glengarry Glen Ross*: "They asked me for a favor. I said, the real favor, follow my advice and fire your fucking ass, because a loser is a loser!" OK, maybe that's a bit harsh. But you get my point.

Saying what needs to be said in an authentic and memorable way is what the charisma of transparency is all about.

Picture this: a CEO steps onto the stage at an annual shareholders' meeting. She has to share the news of an unexpected financial shortfall, a situation that would usually trigger unease among stakeholders. However, with her charisma, she captures her audience's attention, leads them through the intricacies of the setback, and delivers the news in a way that rises above the issue—makes it not about them or her but about transparency on where they are together on the issue. Transparency allows both parties to align on the future, beyond the issue. This is the charisma of transparency in action—making the concept of transparency engaging, impactful, and trust-building.

Transparency, while certainly challenging to keep up consistently, forms the bedrock of trust within organizations and with clients. This means you need to "own it"—hold yourself accountable for the entire spectrum of outcomes, the victories, and the setbacks. Owning the good and the bad involves an open acknowledgment of success and failure.

An interesting aspect of transparency lies in its relationship with emotional detachment. When we wholeheartedly commit to transparency, we tend to dissociate from the emotional burden that both positive and negative outcomes can bear. It's like buying a Diet Coke at a gas station for ninety-nine cents, where we don't really think about the tax that brings the total to a buck.09 (just watch the movie). Similarly, transparency allows us to bypass the emotional turmoil tied to frank conversations about performance.

On the roller-coaster ride of entrepreneurship, mistakes will happen. Transparency means openly admitting these mistakes. Which means validating them, owning them. These situations might involve your team or clients, but the approach to handling these issues is what sets a great leader apart from the pack. There's profound value in owning up to a mistake with a client rather than evading responsibility. Honesty like that is not only a testament to your integrity but also resonates with customers.

We are all human beings prone to mistakes. As leaders, when we recognize and openly admit our fallibility, we draw empathy from clients who are also prone to errors. This shared vulnerability often strengthens the relationship with customers, establishing a deeper sense of trust and honesty.

A successful leader combines honesty with empathy, transparency with accountability, which, in turn, builds trust and respect.

Transparency oftentimes serves as a mirror, reflecting our humanity in our professional roles. The concept of "fake it till you make it" shouldn't translate to a facade of perfection but rather a transparent journey of continuous learning and growth. This is the authentic path to success—learning, evolving, and being open about it at every step.

The charisma of transparency lies not just in acknowledging and owning mistakes but in the style and grace of being open. A successful leader combines honesty with empathy, transparency with accountability, which, in turn, builds trust and respect.

But beyond that charisma, there are substantial, tangible benefits that come with embracing transparency in every facet of business.

The Benefits of Transparency

When a last-minute technical glitch threatened to delay the release of a new product, the CEO had a choice to make—either hide the problem and go ahead with the planned launch, which would risk the company's reputation, or be transparent about the issue with all stakeholders.

Choosing the latter path, she emailed every customer about the delay, explained the issue, and offered a sincere apology. The response from the customers was overwhelming. They appreciated the honesty, even expressing a deeper trust in the company because of her transparency. This instance is a testament to the power of transparency in building trust, loyalty, and commitment within the business ecosystem.

Transparency has a unique role in shaping lasting relationships within a company, its clients, and stakeholders. By fostering an environment of open communication, transparency lays a strong foundation for trust and loyalty. As a result, clients and stakeholders become more invested in your company's success.

For Alpine Intel, transparency has always played a key role in strengthening client relationships. By being forthright about the hurdles, setbacks, and mistakes, I've consistently found that our clients appreciated the honesty. That level of openness helped forge a bond of trust and mutual respect.

Internally, transparency starts by being candid with your team, establishing clear expectations, and providing honest feedback. Transparency has always been baked into our performance management system, even when we lacked the tools and technology to track it. We are deliberate about building our processes in granular integration with our technology systems so employees are always in the know, by the minute, about their performance metrics, and they know exactly where they stand regarding their goals and tasks. This type of transparency has turned our company into a well-oiled machine, with employees becoming self-managers and reducing the need for excessive supervision or micromanagement.

Such an environment of transparency within a team frees up time for focusing on core tasks and responsibilities. It minimizes unnecessary back-and-forths and dispels ambiguity, allowing everyone to concentrate on their respective roles. There's a profound sense of relief in knowing you can dedicate your attention to your duties without being distracted by confusion or miscommunication. This live and in-the-moment performance measurement isn't for everyone, and I'm fine with that. They don't have to go home; they just can't work here.

Here are a few other ways in which transparency makes you better:

- **Improves Decision-Making:** With transparent processes and data sharing, team members have all the necessary information to make informed decisions. This can significantly enhance the effectiveness and efficiency of decision-making within an organization.

- **Encourages Innovation:** When employees have full visibility into the workings of the organization, they are more likely to suggest improvements and innovations. They can see the larger picture and understand how their roles fit within it.

- **Boosts Employee Morale:** Transparency fosters a sense of fairness and equality within an organization. When employees feel that they are being treated with honesty, their job satisfaction and morale are likely to increase.

- **Enhances Customer Relationships:** Customers appreciate businesses that are honest and open with them. Transparency can lead to stronger customer relationships and increased customer loyalty.

- **Mitigates Crises:** In times of crises, a transparent approach can help control the narrative and manage the fallout. Companies that are open about their issues tend to recover faster and maintain stronger stakeholder relationships.

- **Attracts Talent:** In today's job market, candidates value a transparent work culture. Companies that are open about their operations, culture, and values can attract high-quality talent.

- **Promotes Accountability:** Transparency ensures all actions and decisions made within a company are open for scrutiny. This promotes a culture of accountability, where everyone understands that their actions have implications.

- **Drives Continuous Improvement:** With a transparent environment, mistakes are identified and addressed, not hidden. This promotes a culture of continuous learning and improvement.

- **Reputation Management:** Transparency helps build and maintain a positive reputation in the market. It signals to stakeholders, competitors, and customers that the company operates with honesty and integrity.

- **Increases Productivity:** When information is shared openly, it saves time that would otherwise be spent in seeking approvals or clarifications. This can improve the overall productivity of the team.

In essence, transparency is the secret sauce that builds trust, loyalty, and commitment within your company. It's a catalyst for stronger relationships, better teamwork, and, ultimately, a thriving, resilient business. Transparency is not just a buzzword—it's a game-changer. By paying the transparency tax, delivering information with charisma, and embracing openness, you can build trust, loyalty, and commitment inside and outside of your company.

So go ahead, be transparent, and watch your business thrive like never before. After all, transparency is not just a fairy tale, but it's your competitive advantage in the real world of business, as well.

A Fairy Tale about Transparency

Once upon a time, in the land of Damondia, there was a bustling marketplace where merchants from all corners of the kingdom would gather to sell their wares. Among them was a young and ambitious merchant named Lucas Jr., who had dreams of becoming the most successful trader in all the realm.

Lucas Jr. was known for his charming smile and silver-tongue. He had a knack for persuading customers to buy his products, even if they didn't necessarily need them. While his business thrived, Lucas Jr. had a secret. He would often engage in deceptive practices, hiding the true quality and origins of his goods. He believed that transparency was unnecessary and that his customers would never find out.

One day, a wise old woman named Elara visited the marketplace. She possessed a unique ability to see through falsehoods and read people's true intentions. As she strolled through the stalls, her piercing gaze fell upon Lucas Jr. Sensing his deceitful ways, Elara approached him with a gentle smile.

"Dear Lucas Junior, you pitiful turd," she said, her voice carrying the weight of wisdom. "Transparency is the essence of trust in business. By revealing the truth behind your products, you create a bond of integrity with your customers, ensuring their loyalty for years to come."

Lucas Jr. scoffed at her words, dismissing them as mere ramblings of an old woman. He continued with his deceitful practices, blind to the consequences that awaited him. As fate would have it, news of Lucas Jr.'s deceptive ways reached the ears of the kingdom's ruler, Queen Isabella. Determined to uphold justice and fairness, she summoned Lucas Jr. to her palace.

Standing before the queen, Lucas Jr. trembled, realizing that his actions had caught up with him. Queen Isabella's eyes gleamed with a mix of disappointment and resolve.

"Lucas Junior, I have always believed in giving everyone a fair chance," she spoke firmly. "But trust, once broken, is difficult to mend. Your lack of transparency has tarnished your reputation and betrayed the trust of your customers."

But Queen Isabella didn't banish Lucas Jr. from the kingdom or even punish him. Instead, she offered him a second chance—an opportunity to redeem himself. She explained that by embracing transparency and practicing honesty, Lucas Jr. could rebuild the trust he had lost.

Overwhelmed with gratitude and remorse, Lucas Jr. realized the significance of Queen Isabella's offer. He vowed to change his ways and embarked on a journey of self-improvement. But it was too fucking late.

The old, wise woman, Elara, had already shouted from the rooftops that Lucas Jr. was a lying turd, and his merchandise was nothing but a bunch of knock-offs. The townspeople rushed the castle, dragged Lucas Jr. screaming and kicking to the top of the highest parapet, lit him ablaze, and then tossed his writhing body into the alligator-infested moat below.

By being transparent, Elara earned the trust of the townspeople. She took over the lease for Lucas Jr.'s shop and, within two years, expanded into dozens of other kingdoms, living transparently ever after.

Reflections Make You Better

As businesses navigate the landscape of the twenty-first century, transparency has become an essential attribute for success. However, just like freedom, transparency comes at a cost. Here are some strategies and best practices to navigate the complexities of transparency while mitigating its associated tax:

- **Build Trust:** Be open, honest, and forthcoming to establish trust with your team, clients, and stakeholders.
- **Foster Loyalty:** Transparency creates loyalty as people appreciate the authenticity and integrity it represents.
- **Cultivate Commitment:** When you're transparent about goals, challenges, and decision-making, you inspire commitment from your team and stakeholders.
- **Prioritize Communication:** Develop strong communication skills to deliver transparency with charisma and engage your audience effectively.
- **Create a Culture of Openness:** Encourage transparency as a core value, and create an environment where honesty and open dialogue are celebrated.
- **Embrace the Freedom:** Let go of guilt and uncertainty by being transparent, allowing you to focus on what truly matters.
- **Lead by Example:** Be transparent yourself, and set the tone for transparency in your company.
- **Be Receptive to Feedback:** Encourage open feedback, and actively listen to create a culture of trust and collaboration.
- **Make Transparency a Competitive Advantage:** Stand out from the crowd by embracing transparency as a differentiating factor in your industry.
- **Believe in the Power of Transparency:** Let go of skepticism, and embrace transparency as a transformative force that can make your company better.

ELIEVE IN BETTER / THE EVOLUTION OF CORE PRINCIPLES
HAT PIONEERED AN INDUSTRY // AUTHENTICITY MAKES
OU BETTER // BELIEVE IN BETTER / THE EVOLUTION
F CORE PRINCIPLES THAT PIONEERED AN INDUSTRY //
USTLING MAKES YOU BETTER // BELIEVE IN BETTER /
HE EVOLUTION OF CORE PRINCIPLES THAT PIONEERED AN
NDUSTRY // BELIEVE IN BETTER / THE EVOLUTION OF CORE
RINCIPLES THAT PIONEERED AN INDUSTRY // SELLING
AKES YOU BETTER // BELIEVE IN BETTER / THE EVOLUTION
F CORE PRINCIPLES THAT PIONEERED AN INDUSTRY //
ELIEVE IN BETTER / THE EVOLUTION OF CORE PRINCIPLES
HAT PIONEERED AN INDUSTRY // BELIEVE IN BETTER /
HE EVOLUTION OF CORE PRINCIPLES THAT PIONEERED AN
NDUSTRY // BELIEVE IN BETTER / THE EVOLUTION OF CORE
RINCIPLES THAT PIONEERED AN INDUSTRY // UNDERSTANDING
ERSPECTIVE MAKES YOU BETTER //BELIEVE IN BETTER /
HE EVOLUTION OF CORE PRINCIPLES THAT PIONEERED AN
NDUSTRY // BELIEVE IN BETTER / THE EVOLUTION OF CORE
RINCIPLES THAT PIONEERED AN INDUSTRY // TEAMWORK
AKES YOU BETTER // BELIEVE IN BETTER / THE EVOLUTION
F CORE PRINCIPLES THAT PIONEERED AN INDUSTRY //
AKING ACTION MAKES YOU BETTER // BELIEVE IN BETTER
 THE EVOLUTION OF CORE PRINCIPLES THAT PIONEERED AN
NDUSTRY // TRANSPARENCY MAKES YOU BETTER // BELIEVE
N BETTER / THE EVOLUTION OF CORE PRINCIPLES THAT
IONEERED AN INDUSTRY // DRIVING PROFITABILITY MAKES
OU BETTER // THE EVOLUTION OF CORE PRINCIPLES THAT
IONEERED AN INDUSTRY // PROCESS MAKES YOU BETTER //
ELIEVE IN BETTER / THE EVOLUTION OF CORE PRINCIPLES
HAT PIONEERED AN INDUSTRY // CHANGE MAKES YOU BETTER
 / BELIEVE IN BETTER / THE EVOLUTION OF CORE PRINCIPLE

BELIEVE IN BETTER / THE EVOLUTION OF CORE PRINCIPLE
THAT PIONEERED AN INDUSTRY // AUTHENTICITY MAKE
YOU BETTER // BELIEVE IN BETTER / THE EVOLUTIO
OF CORE PRINCIPLES THAT PIONEERED AN INDUSTRY /
HUSTLING MAKES YOU BETTER // BELIEVE IN BETTER
THE EVOLUTION OF CORE PRINCIPLES THAT PIONEERED A
INDUSTRY // BELIEVE IN BETTER / THE EVOLUTION OF COR
PRINCIPLES THAT PIONEERED AN INDUSTRY // SELLIN
MAKES YOU BETTER // BELIEVE IN BETTER / THE EVOLUTIO
OF CORE PRINCIPLES THAT PIONEERED AN INDUSTRY /
BELIEVE IN BETTER / THE EVOLUTION OF CORE PRINCIPLE
THAT PIONEERED AN INDUSTRY // BELIEVE IN BETTER
THE EVOLUTION OF CORE PRINCIPLES THAT PIONEERED A
INDUSTRY // BELIEVE IN BETTER / THE EVOLUTION OF COR
PRINCIPLES THAT PIONEERED AN INDUSTRY // UNDERSTANDIN
PERSPECTIVE MAKES YOU BETTER //BELIEVE IN BETTER
THE EVOLUTION OF CORE PRINCIPLES THAT PIONEERED A
INDUSTRY // BELIEVE IN BETTER / THE EVOLUTION OF COR
PRINCIPLES THAT PIONEERED AN INDUSTRY // TEAMWOR
MAKES YOU BETTER // BELIEVE IN BETTER / THE EVOLUTIO
OF CORE PRINCIPLES THAT PIONEERED AN INDUSTRY /
TAKING ACTION MAKES YOU BETTER // BELIEVE IN BETTE
/ THE EVOLUTION OF CORE PRINCIPLES THAT PIONEERE
AN INDUSTRY // TRANSPARENCY MAKES YOU BETTER /
BELIEVE IN BETTER / THE EVOLUTION OF CORE PRINCIPLES
THAT PIONEERED AN INDUSTRY // **PROFITABILITY MAKES
YOU BETTER** // THE EVOLUTION OF CORE PRINCIPLES THA
PIONEERED AN INDUSTRY // PROCESS MAKES YOU BETTER /
BELIEVE IN BETTER / THE EVOLUTION OF CORE PRINCIPLES
THAT PIONEERED AN INDUSTRY // CHANGE MAKES YOU BETTE
// BELIEVE IN BETTER / THE EVOLUTION OF CORE PRINCIPLE

Profitability Makes You Better

Business is all about solving people's problems—at a profit.

—PAUL MARSDEN

Who doesn't love a good, old-fashioned tale of misplaced priorities?

Imagine you have a business partner, a perfectly capable executive who is equally responsible for generating revenue. The problem is, this guy is more interested in enjoying the spoils of success than actually working for them—more focused on the color of the office carpet than the color of the balance sheet. A guy who gets excited by cruising around with real estate brokers, being the proverbial "big shot," instead of crunching numbers and closing deals. Now, this is not a jab at any particular two people in my past (OK, maybe it is); rather it's a poignant illustration of a glaring problem I see far too often in the business world.

We all know the mantra that business has always been about profitability. Novel idea, I know. The problem is, a lot of leaders fail to realize profitability is a journey, not a destination. You may reach profitability, but to stay there, you need to keep adapting, keep innovating, and keep hustling.

In today's start-up landscape, particularly in the high-stakes arenas of mergers and acquisitions (M&A), venture capital, and

The problem is, a lot of leaders fail to realize profitability is a journey, not a destination.

private equity, the importance of profit often gets tossed aside like last year's failed remake of an '80s movie. The reality is that some of these financial firms are focused on the *top line*, because the ability for the next guy to create profit from expense/cost synergies, making the product more profitable, is sometimes what they are selling. "Aw shucks, I guess you guys are smarter than me. You can make this business into a ten-times larger business from an EBITDA standpoint, so buy it from me for five times what I bought it for and you can keep the change!"

Generating revenue isn't rocket science. It's about solving problems. Period. It's about creating an urgency that stimulates buying decisions and shortens sales cycles because, at the end of the day, all roads (or at least the ones we're interested in for purposes of this chapter) lead to profit.

Too many times I've seen brilliant ideas disintegrate because someone forgot to ask the million-dollar question: Would any insurance carriers want to buy this? If so, what is the length of the sales cycle? I see the wreckage of such oversight scattered across the landscape of InsurTech.

Profitability is the lifeblood of a company. It is what allows businesses to grow, to innovate, to venture into new territories. Profitability is not a sprint; it's a marathon of dedication. It involves being dedicated to defining processes that you live by, enabling technology for efficiency, automating what can be automated, and making data-driven decisions. It's about creating task and workflow approvals to eliminate needless touchpoints on transactions. But above all, it's about constructing your operations to drive profit.

Change management is the real impact-driver here, even though it might not be as popular as innovation and tech development. It's a tough pill to swallow because change is often uncomfortable and almost always met with resistance in my world. But it's this very dedication to change, to improve, that drives efficiency, leading to profit.

Sure, there are those out there who argue that the CEO having a granular understanding and focus on individual transactions is shortsighted, but I wholeheartedly disagree. The accumulation of these transactions crafts our business narrative. Create a profitable product that people want to buy, and you've set up a self-sustaining cycle. A well-thought-out operation, built on process and standardization, runs itself, fulfills customer service-level agreements (SLAs), and is the catalyst for scaling. Do that right, and everything else falls into place.

The thing is, once you hit profitability, the real work begins: understanding what drives it. It might not be as glamorous as choosing carpet colors for a new office or basking in the spotlight of real estate negotiations, but it's the nuts and bolts that keep the business machine running.

Because it's one thing to become profitable, but the real magic lies in sustaining and growing that profitability. And to understand how to sustain and grow, we need to get back to some basic principles of profitability.

Revenue 101

If revenue is the lifeblood of a business, the heartbeat is talking to customers. Seems simple, doesn't it? The important things usually are.

One of my most successful companies was born out of this simple concept. You see, one day, I decided to do something unheard of—I sat down and listened to a customer. I mean, *really* listened. And guess what? They told me what to build. It was as if they laid out a blueprint in front of me, not just for a product but also for a profitable business venture. They said, "Damon, my real problem is over here." And just like that, it clicked.

How many times do we miss these opportunities? We march into meetings, armed with our features, benefits, and value propositions, but often forget that we're there to solve a problem for the customer. We need to remember that, at times, salespeople aren't always empowered to invent new products on the spot. But they should be conduits, feeding back information to leadership about what the customer truly needs.

Now, this doesn't mean you deviate from your overarching business model and go from InsurTech to a taco franchise just because a customer asked you to. You need to stick to the fundamentals of what makes you the best in the world at something. In Jim Collins's book *Good to Great*, Jim describes the difference between the fox and the hedgehog. The fox has a thousand ways to try to get at the hedgehog to eat him, but the hedgehog only needs to be good at one thing—rolling into a ball.

This might seem like an obvious strategy, but you'd be surprised how many businesses derail from it, especially at critical inflection points. As businesses grow, there's this overwhelming pressure to reinvent the wheel, to do something radically new to impress your shareholders or beat the competition. But this is where many businesses go seriously wrong.

These inflection points are real, and if not navigated carefully, they can crush a company. You've built your success on certain principles, products, or services. To deviate drastically from this path, especially when you're scaling, is like trying to swim upstream while juggling flaming ducks—it's exhausting and risky, and there's a strong likelihood you'll either get burned or shit on.

The common issue I see within M&A is that founders who have been acquired by private equity are suddenly in the business of private equity. From the $1 million earnings before interest, taxes, depreciation, and amortization (EBITDA) business all the way up scale, many people who receive majority recaps in private equity—a.k.a. no longer have control of their company—a.k.a. sold out—a.k.a. dropped the mic—a.k.a. owned by someone else—a.k.a. not qualified to create a pipeline of prospects for acquisitions, or introductory meetings with acquisitions, or negotiate acquisitions, or be anywhere close to a closing table for an acquisition, or create an investment thesis on a roll up of acquisitions, or create a strategic integration for acquisitions, or speak on behalf of shareholders of large institutional and private equity funds, somehow feel empowered to "buy and sell companies." Who the fuck do you think you are? What the fuck do you think this is? Are you now Stephen Schwarzman or Richard Branson? Hey Bud Fox, let's watch a movie from the fucking 2000s at least.

Take the money, and go to Florida or whatever it is you want to do, and just get out of the way of the professionals. Or even better, take the obligation of rollover investment seriously, and go grow the business that you know how to grow.

Private equity is incredibly hard. And there is a reason that the PE firm responsible for your success sometimes makes you feel like a fraud when speaking about investment and financial topics. Because they are incredibly intelligent, and it took years to gain their kind of perspective. When founders and CEOs turn into PE geniuses, the moment they get their first big check, they are unknowingly making a mockery of private equity to the shareholders who just made a big bet on them.

Does it sound like I'm venting? Good, because I am. I know all of this from experience. There was a moment where I fell into this category. I've even dipped my toe back a couple of times getting caught up in the hype of acquisitions as the only fast, easy, best way to grow. Does M&A have a place? Absolutely! Best strategy? Maybe! But you as a founder who just got scooped up by PE are not qualified without serious support by your team and PE group. And you damn well better have a good investment thesis before you burn the remains of the ever-dimming time in your career chasing the next great bet.

Remember, you're not private equity—you're you. The best value that you can add as a CEO, owner, or founder is that your product or service and industrial knowledge of your niche, or industry, or customers, or data science are what make you great. An acquisition has to both run and grow following the prestigious acquisition paperwork signed, you fucking prat. You can actually be the person to help identify what needs to happen (based on your industry knowledge and institutional knowledge of whatever it is your company does) to help accelerate that growth. Here's a trick: just imagine all of the hype and prestige of buying and selling companies that you absorb from attorneys and consultants, and all the dads in your Boy Scout group and country club, as nothing more than administrative work. Because, by the way, *it is*. It's lending! It's leverage on revenue expectations, based on a profit requirement, and

If you find yourself in a gold mine, don't start digging for silver.

also on future growth that must be obtained and you must commit to, or shit hits the fan. M&A is administrative work in banking, lending, and legal and for consultant groups and accountants. If you want to let your ego down a little bit, just view these M&A transactions as what they really are, administrative in function. By the way, if you are an insurance services company considering a sale—we are in the market— please send info so that our deal team can get engaged and evaluate the opportunity. Seriously.

All that to say, stick with what you know, to what made your business successful in the first place. If you're good at making widgets, then by all means, continue making the best damn widgets the world has ever seen. Will you learn about M&A along the way and eventually have the skills in this department? Maybe, if you make some profit, listen, and engage when you are presented acquisition opportunities. But seriously, leave the M&A to the M&A folks.

Profitability is certainly a cause for celebration. But revenue also equals *responsibility*.

The essence here is to keep things simple, to remember the basics of what brought you profitability in the first place. Bottom line, if you find yourself in a gold mine, don't start digging for silver.

But there's another essential element of sustaining revenue—the holy trinity of profitability. This is where the worlds of people, process, and technology collide, in the most productive way possible.

The Profitability Triangle

OK, let's address the white elephant in the room. Yes, making revenue is exciting. Profitability is certainly a cause for celebration. But revenue also equals *responsibility*. Profitability isn't about buying flashy office suites or throwing lavish parties. It's about building a legacy business, not a lifestyle business.

That means once the confetti has settled, it's time to get back to work. Invest your profits back into your business. Back to the people, processes, and technology that make the magic happen—the Profitability Triangle. Because believe it or not, generating revenue is the easy part. How you spend it is what truly matters.

First up, people. And I don't mean just any people. I'm talking about the folks who aren't afraid to get their hands dirty—the ones who are embedded in the transaction, those who understand and can enhance the core product. These are the not-so-glamorous hires that no one wants to talk about, but trust me, they're the ones who matter the most. They're the technical wizards, the product savants—the ones who can pick up the phone and answer it exactly as you would. Find executives who can get their hands dirty like I have a few times, and you have yourself a unicorn.

Then comes process. As you scale, you need to have robust processes in place and stick to them no matter what! These will help you fulfill your product deliverables and ensure you aren't wrestling with the same problems over and over again.

And finally, technology or product. In this day and age, if you're not investing in technology to enable your business processes (key word here is *enable*), you're getting left behind. But remember, technology is only as good as the people who create and manage it. And the processes that the tech is built on. So make sure you hire those who not only understand your product but also know how to build the technology that will support your scaling efforts.

In the early stages of business, you might find yourself funneling most of your profit back into hiring the best talent—the folks who will roll up their sleeves and help you scale from a $2 million venture to a $10 million juggernaut. But as you hit those inflection points, your focus needs to shift. It's no longer just about the people—it's about formalizing processes and refining your product (technology).

The point is, profitability isn't just about making money—it's also about using that money to continually improve and grow.

Profitability isn't just about making money—it's also about using that money to continually improve and grow.

It's worth noting, however, that sometimes the best way to move forward is by letting go.

Let Go to Get a Better Grip

If you're anything like me—a hard-charging entrepreneur who's launched several businesses—you probably find it incredibly difficult to release control. You're familiar with every tiny detail, every wrinkle and wart of your operation. After all, who else could possibly handle the tasks the way you do? Here's a hard pill to swallow for most successful leaders—keeping your hands in every single aspect of your business doesn't actually add to its profitability. In fact, it often has the opposite effect.

I ran my business, foot on the gas, for eight grueling years, investing my sweat equity into its growth. Looking back, I can definitely see that I clung to some roles for too long. Was it because I loved doing them? Because I believed no one else could do them well? Because I found it challenging to hire the right people? Probably a combination of all three.

The ultimate goal for any entrepreneur should be to shift from working *in* the business to working *on* the business. Sure, it's an overused phrase, but it's overused for a reason—because it's freaking true. And getting there requires a necessary exercise in ego deflation. You need to understand that *anyone* can do your job if given the right guidance.

Write down the processes, the decision-making criteria, the nuances, and the exceptions. Spell it out, step-by-step. Once you do this, you'll see that the tasks you're so fiercely protective of can be handled by others. And those supposed exceptions you think only you can manage? Those are rarer than you might imagine.

Profitability isn't just about the dollars flowing into the bank. It's also about the value each team member brings to the table, including you.

Take a moment to look at the cost of *you*, the entrepreneur, holding on to certain roles. Factor in your value and the opportunity cost. Suppose you could be focusing on strategic growth instead of troubleshooting customer service issues. Isn't that a better use of your time?

As the CEO, your role has an intrinsic value that adds to the company's profitability. By occupying yourself with tasks that could be better handled by others, you're inadvertently reducing that value. It's like a five-star general in the US Army digging foxholes; sure, they would probably be great at it, but wouldn't their time be better spent strategizing? Once again, I am in no way shape or form saying what I do (or CEOs like me) is equivalent to the dedication and sacrifice required to become a five-star general. But the underlying principle of proper resource allocation is the same.

Profitability isn't just about the dollars flowing into the bank. It's also about the value each team member brings to the table, including you. So go ahead, let go. You might just find that you'll get a better grip on what's truly important—increasing profitability, creating a legacy, and, most critical of all, scaling.

The Recipe for Scaling

What the hell is *scaling*, anyway? It's a term thrown around as liberally as the foam on your skinny vanilla latte.

The truth is, scaling your business is more like creating a soup recipe for a handful of people and then realizing you need to make the same soup for a party of five hundred. It's not just a matter of multiplying the number of carrots and adding a dash more salt. It's about comprehending how each ingredient interacts with the others, how it will impact the flavor, the texture, and the overall appeal of your soup. It's understanding the quantity and quality of your ingredients, the timing, and the temperature.

Think of your company as that soup. Each ingredient represents a different aspect of your business—your people, processes, products, technology, marketing strategies, customer service, and so on. And just like with the soup, you need to know each ingredient intimately.

What role does it play? How does it interact with the other ingredients? How does it change the overall result?

It's the understanding of these elements, how they fit together, that allows you to scale with confidence. No intimidation, no fear of the unknown, because you've rolled up your sleeves and made the soup from scratch. You know the taste of the carrot, the crunch of the celery, the aroma of the onion powder—you know your soup and you know your business.

If you remember anything, remember this: Scaling doesn't mean just making more widgets. It means understanding your business at its most granular level and then expanding that understanding.

If you remember anything, remember this: Scaling doesn't mean just making more widgets. It means understanding your business at its most granular level and then expanding that understanding. It means preparing the soup for five, then for fifty, then for five hundred, always adjusting, always tasting, always perfecting. It means being willing to learn from your customers, your team, and the ongoing process and always striving to create a better bowl of soup.

In your quest for profitability, don't forget that the business that scales successfully is the business that understands the recipe of its success. Don't just throw ingredients together hoping for the best. Master your recipe, and then scale it.

But profitability and success aren't just about generating revenue and scaling. It's also about giving back, sharing our experiences, and helping others reach their potential. In the same way we've nurtured and grown our businesses, we have the opportunity to cultivate a culture of giving. It's like adding a secret ingredient to our soup recipe that makes it worthy of inclusion in a Michelin-starred restaurant.

Pay It Forward

The importance of the human element in a successful business operation cannot be overstated. I remember pondering about where to put my money in terms of investment. One decision I made was to invest in leadership. I could almost hear you gasp there. *Invest in leadership? How does that work?* Well, it does involve equity, it does involve profit, and yes, it does involve giving away or, should I say, strategically placing your hard-earned success into the hands of others.

That's the thing about holding on too tight. It's like squeezing sand in your palm; the tighter you squeeze, the more it slips away. I've seen people hold on to everything and run their businesses like a fortress with them as the lonely king. No doubt, that works for some. But for me, my path led me to share my success, to delegate, to trust. To pay it forward.

I invested in partners and handed them a slice of the pie. And they weren't just any partners, mind you. They were the ones who put in the sweat, the toil, and the time and helped build the business from the ground up. The result? Well, let's just say, they became millionaires ten times over, thanks to our collective success.

Did I ever worry I was making a mistake? Sure. What if you invest in the wrong people? That's a valid concern. But the secret sauce in our proverbial soup is taking that leap of faith. Sure, there are risks involved, but the rewards are even sweeter. And you accomplish far more together than alone. Don't just look at it as giving away your equity but as catalyzing an environment of shared success, an environment where your team has a stake in what they're building. Because when you create this sense of shared ownership, people are more driven, more engaged, and more determined to see the business succeed.

When you pay it forward, you're not only investing in the present, but you're also sculpting the future. Investing in people and paying it forward are indeed a vital part of building a profitable business. But this doesn't end there. It lays the foundation for an even more critical aspect of business success—building a solid team that shares your vision and contributes to your journey.

Build Your Team

On the journey of constructing a successful and profitable business, one of the inevitable decisions you face is about building your C-suite—that glamorous group of executives who have the power to either take your business to dizzying heights or, well, not. You may have come across a surprising statistic that the CFO is often the last member to be appointed in this prestigious suite. Hard to believe, especially given that they're the ones playing watchdog over the financial health of the company. But most leaders are loathe to relin-

Your job is to work yourself out of a job.

quish that financial control to a virtual stranger unless they absolutely have to.

I brought on board our CFO not at the very beginning, not when we were a small team trying to find our footing. I waited until we were at an inflection point, a point where a CFO was not a luxury but a necessity. Before that, it felt like playing make-believe business, with a CFO role that was more ornamental than functional.

However, let me clarify something—it's not about the role or the title. It's about the system and the processes. Our business, at its most basic, was a cycle of "get the claims, send the report, rinse and repeat." And if your system is well-designed and robust, even a mammoth task like accounting should seamlessly blend into your operations rather than being an end-of-period pain in the ass.

This ties back to another principle I live by: if all the institutional knowledge lives within a single person, you're setting yourself up for a fall. Let's say your CFO is the only one who understands the financial maze of your business. Or your sales rep is the only one who has built relationships with your clients. That's a precarious position to be in. The key is to make sure that the knowledge, the know-how, the Intellectual Property (IP), resides within the organization, not an individual. And yes, that goes for me and you, too!

> **If all the institutional knowledge lives within a single person, you're setting yourself up for a fall.**

I frequently tell my team, "Your job is to work yourself out of your job." If you're growing and everyone is striving to make their roles obsolete by streamlining and optimizing, there's a limitless buffet of responsibilities waiting for you.

The idea is to let go. And once you do, it's liberating. You realize that the fear of the sales rep walking away with the accounts, or the CFO withholding vital financial knowledge, was just that—fear. By infusing the knowledge into the enterprise, you're setting up your business for genuine scalability.

And what's the alternative? If you allow your executives to hoard knowledge, they can effectively hold your business hostage, demanding a king's ransom for their services. Suddenly, you're not leading the organization anymore but being led by it.

Hostage Situation

Hostage situations can happen right within your business walls. You might not have a twocker kitted out with a piece demanding your wallet, but you may have a department, a team, or even an individual holding your profitability hostage.

Let's consider one area where this happens frequently: development—those tech wizards who make your vision a digital reality. Now, don't get me wrong, they are brilliant at what they do, but here's the catch: if you're not careful, you can easily lose control of your own product.

Imagine this. You have an idea, but it's not fully formed yet. So, you walk up to your development team and say, "Hey, I want to do this." They nod, smile, and get to work. And what do they build? Well, they build what they want to build. Why? Because you haven't given them clear expectations. And in the absence of those, you've handed them the power and put a metaphorical gun to your own head.

What happens next is a sequence of spiraling costs, unclear processes, and a product that's held together by the whims of your development team. One company I came across had sixty developers with an annual maintenance cost of $30 million! Why? Because they had outsourced their knowledge and handed over their IP without understanding how their product actually worked.

In effect, they were pouring money into an unknown entity. And guess what? They had no choice. It was a hostage situation of their own creation, and they were paying up their lunch money every single day.

It's like garnishing your soup with a dollop of some special cilantro-lime sour cream that customers absolutely love. But the catch is, you don't know that recipe. And the vendor, smirking at the popularity, ups the cost, knowing you're now at their mercy. It's a situation where your costs are now outpacing your profitability.

So, the question becomes, how do you avoid being held hostage by your own business? The secret lies in thorough due diligence. Not just operational IT diligence but also the mapping of technology to your operational processes. You should be able to see how your sales team, accounting, marketing campaigns, and customer return on investment (ROI) map to your technology.

If this alignment isn't apparent, or if your development team can't explain it to you, beware! You may be walking into a hostage situation without even knowing it. And trust me, there's nothing worse than being held captive in your own business.

So, make sure that dollop of cilantro-lime sour cream enhances your soup rather than emptying your pocket. The recipe to avoid a hostage situation is clear expectations, due diligence, and a solid understanding of how your tech aligns with your operations.

The recipe to avoid a hostage situation is clear expectations, due diligence, and a solid understanding of how your tech aligns with your operations.

But what happens when the tables turn? What if you find yourself on the other side of the equation, holding the metaphorical gun? At some point, the tables do flip. The business hostage scenario is not a one-way street. In fact, let's say you're the one creating the proprietary ingredient in our soup analogy—that dollop of cilantro-lime sour cream. You must protect that recipe as if your life depends on it, because guess what? The life of your business does. This isn't just about money. This isn't just your revenue growth pathway. It's your identity.

Remember, your unique selling proposition, that thing which sets you apart, is your sour cream recipe. If you've found that sweet spot where other companies can't quite figure out how to recreate your magic, then you're sitting on a gold mine.

You can dictate your price for that sour cream as long as your customers see the value you're providing. You don't expose your secret ingredients or disclose where you source your key limes from. Your exclusivity is your power, and your power is your profitability.

And yes, relationships in business are important. So, as you protect your sour cream recipe, remember to maintain healthy relationships with your clients and vendors. Strive to strike a balance where you remain profitable, and they see the value in what you provide.

But here's a word of caution: If you ever find yourself in a business relationship that begins to eat into your profits and starts affecting your margins negatively, it's time for a pivot. If that dollop of sour cream becomes a bone of contention, it's time to innovate. Perhaps it's time to go from soup to sandwiches or introduce a new product altogether that your customers will adore.

In the game of profitability, adaptation and innovation are your best friends. Remember, you're the master of your own destiny. Hold that power with grace, protect your uniqueness, and continue to add value to your customers. That's how you stay on the other side of the gun, where you call the shots.

Now, staying on the right side of the profitability gun—at its core—means having stellar customer service. But that doesn't mean the customer is always right.

The Customer Is *Not* Always Right

Yeah, I said it. Heresy, you say? Not really. Because great leaders need to juggle customer satisfaction and profitability at the same time. But it means walking a fine line. Alec Baldwin's character, Blake, in *Glengarry Glen Ross* said, "They're sitting out there waiting to give you their money. Are you gonna take it?" A slightly modified version that I tell my team all the time is our customers are *trying* to give us their money. We just need to be smart about taking it.

The key lies in not losing focus on your core product while satisfying a customer's need. You see, scaling is an art, and it's painted on a canvas of consistency. Sure, we can incorporate customer requests but only in an automated way that allows the operation to run smoothly, such as a well-oiled assembly line.

What happens when a customer asks for a change, for something that may threaten to clog up the machine? It depends. What's their role in the customer's company? Are they in a position to even make such a request? Often, operational processes are tweaked because one customer who barely had any clout to ask for it demanded change. Now imagine you end up doing that for every customer request you receive. Trust me, that's a rabbit hole you do *not* want to go down.

At the end of the day, business is about making sure the customer is satisfied but not at the expense of your profit margins. It's a delicate dance to be sure. So how do you know when to turn down a customer's request? Well, the answer to that is complicated and relies on a ton of variables only you can answer. But one rule of thumb to always follow is to never turn down the revenue faucet so far it impacts your bottom line.

As the saying goes.

A Bird in the Hand

I know, it's another dusty, wrinkled old adage. But it's painfully evergreen in the world of business. When my business was just taking flight, every day felt like chaos—orders pouring in, the phone ringing off the hook, paperwork piling up, and customers demanding attention.

But amid that frenzy, I realized something—just like birds, profits don't fall from the sky. It takes effort, determination, and a hell of a lot of strategy to make them appear. One day, I gave myself a target: bill $10,000 a day. It seemed daunting at first, but this tangible goal gave me a sense of direction. After all, what's the first thing you plug into GPS when you want to get somewhere? That's right, the destination.

By focusing on this goal, I knew I was not only generating revenue but also securing my company's future. It didn't matter if every customer wasn't 100 percent satisfied all the time; I knew I was doing my best to keep the majority happy while still bringing in steady income. And that income is your lifeline. It's what allows you to pay your team, improve your services, and, most important, fight another day.

During one particular hurricane, we had the opportunity to deliver on endless orders that were flooding the emails of our operational management team. What did we do?

Never turn off that revenue faucet. Keep the income coming but not at all costs.

We sent back hundreds of thousands of dollars of orders because we thought smaller transactions later in the hurricane event would be more profitable.

Guess what happened? We didn't take the orders, we didn't get the new orders we had hoped for, and even worse, we turned some customers against us. We pushed back on work we should have been doing.

The lesson: never turn off that revenue faucet. Keep the income coming but not at all costs. Balance is the key, though take a step back and know that you *must* make hay while the sun shines. And while it does, you'd better stock up on benzene-free SPF 70 sunscreen. Although it's not sustainable in the long term, stay up until one o'clock at night if you have to, to deliver on the commitment to your customers.

After all, those guaranteed profits you hold now are far more valuable than the elusive ones you might—or might not—catch in the future.

A Fairy Tale about Profitability

Once upon a time, in the heart of bustling Bazaarville, there was a humble cobbler named Theo. Theo had inherited his father's cobbling shop, *The Happy Heel*—a small, cozy place filled with the fragrance of fresh leather and shoe polish. Despite the shop's name, Theo was anything but happy. The shop barely made enough to pay for the materials, let alone a decent meal for Theo.

One day, a wise old merchant named Eldridge wandered into the shop, seeking refuge from a sudden rainstorm. Eldridge noticed Theo's gloomy disposition and asked what was troubling him. Theo poured out his woes—how his craftsmanship was appreciated, yet he barely made a profit, even though his shoes were sought after in Bazaarville.

Seeing Theo's predicament, Eldridge decided to help. He told Theo about the Golden Rule of Profitability. "Theo," Eldridge said, "you must understand that your shoes' true value isn't just in the materials used, but also in the skill, time, and passion you put into crafting them. This is what makes your shoes unique, and this uniqueness is what your customers value. Raise your prices, and only then will you begin to see the profits you deserve."

The next day, Theo, with some trepidation, followed Eldridge's advice and raised his prices. At first, business slowed. Theo feared he had made a mistake. But soon, word spread about the quality of Theo's shoes, how they lasted longer and fit better than any other in Bazaarville. His customers realized the price was worth it, and business began to boom. Theo was finally making a profit.

One day, a wealthy prince from a neighboring kingdom, known for his extravagant lifestyle, came to Bazaarville. He heard of Theo's famed shoes and decided to order a pair. Ecstatic about serving royalty, Theo worked day and night to create the finest pair of shoes he had ever crafted.

Upon seeing the shoes, the prince was so impressed that he offered to buy Theo's shop and make him the royal shoemaker, offering an amount that would make Theo rich beyond his wildest dreams. Theo eagerly accepted and thus became the royal shoemaker.

Things were great at first. Theo's bank account had more zeroes before the decimal point than he ever thought possible. And he had access to the finest fabrics and materials, to leather harvested from calves that had been rubbed down with baby oil and cream from the day they were born. Then Theo started his first pairs of shoes for the royal family, for the prince's nephew, Mort.

Mort's feet were the worst that Theo had ever encountered in all his decades of being a cobbler. There were slimy corns and warts all over them, and they were badly misshapen, with seven big toes on one foot and four pinkie toes on the other. Unfortunately, Mort's weren't the only ugly feet in the family. As Theo began crafting shoes for other royals, he was blown away by how atrocious their feet were.

And although his bank account was growing, he never got a moment's rest as the entire royal family demanded his attention day and night.

Then one day Theo got on his knees before the prince and asked to be released from his position as the royal cobbler. He had realized that all the money in the world doesn't equal profitability. Profitability also means freedom, the ability to create and innovate, to serve all sorts of customers and live your passion. But it was too fucking late. The prince shook his head and had the castle guards drag Theo back to his royal workshop.

Two days later, Theo got so frustrated from staring at yellowing knobs, pus-filled carbuncles, and toes shaped like curly fries for months on end that he told the prince to take his family's nasty-ass feet and go to the blacksmith to have them fitted with horseshoes.

Needless to say, Theo was tackled to the stone floor by the castle guards and, upon the prince's orders, was flayed alive, tarred and feathered, stuffed in an iron maiden, and then drowned in the royal aquarium where he remains on display to this day for all to enjoy.

What Theo failed to realize early on was that profitability is not just about making money. It's about the freedom that revenue can generate—the freedom to create new and exciting things, to dream and disrupt the industries you are passionate about. The freedom to get rid of the difficult customers and eventually serve only those customers you choose to serve.

Had Theo realized this, he would have lived happily—and profitably—ever after.

Reflections Make You Better

As you move forward, always remember that profitability is not the end goal but a critical factor that fuels growth, innovation, and resilience in your business. It's a journey, not a destination, and every step you take toward enhancing your profitability is a step toward a better, stronger, and more successful business. Here are some key takeaways to help you on your path to building a more profitable and resilient business:

- **Value Your Unique Selling Proposition (USP):** Just like the secret sour cream recipe or Theo's artisanal shoes, your USP is what sets you apart in the market. Protect it, nurture it, and use it to command the price and respect your product or service deserves.

- **Customers Aren't Always Right, but They Are Always Important:** While customer feedback is vital, it's essential to differentiate between whims and valuable suggestions. Never let a single customer's request derail your business's scalability or core operations.

- **Turn Challenges into Opportunities:** Business, much like life, is rarely a smooth ride. But every challenge, every hiccup is an opportunity to learn, adapt, and emerge stronger. Don't be afraid to reassess and adjust your strategy when profitability is at stake.

- **Profitability Is More Than Money:** It's a reflection of your business's health and sustainability. However, remember that the pursuit of profit should not come at the cost of passion and satisfaction derived from your work. Keep the balance to maintain not just a successful business but also a fulfilling life.

- **Keep the Cash Flowing:** Like a bird in hand, having steady, consistent revenue is better than chasing potentially higher but uncertain gains. Keep the faucet of income open, and you'll have a financial buffer to face unexpected challenges.

BELIEVE IN BETTER / THE EVOLUTION OF CORE PRINCIPLES THAT PIONEERED AN INDUSTRY // AUTHENTICITY MAKES YOU BETTER // BELIEVE IN BETTER / THE EVOLUTION OF CORE PRINCIPLES THAT PIONEERED AN INDUSTRY // HUSTLING MAKES YOU BETTER // BELIEVE IN BETTER / THE EVOLUTION OF CORE PRINCIPLES THAT PIONEERED AN INDUSTRY // BELIEVE IN BETTER / THE EVOLUTION OF CORE PRINCIPLES THAT PIONEERED AN INDUSTRY // SELLING MAKES YOU BETTER // BELIEVE IN BETTER / THE EVOLUTION OF CORE PRINCIPLES THAT PIONEERED AN INDUSTRY // BELIEVE IN BETTER / THE EVOLUTION OF CORE PRINCIPLES THAT PIONEERED AN INDUSTRY // BELIEVE IN BETTER / THE EVOLUTION OF CORE PRINCIPLES THAT PIONEERED AN INDUSTRY // BELIEVE IN BETTER / THE EVOLUTION OF CORE PRINCIPLES THAT PIONEERED AN INDUSTRY // UNDERSTANDING PERSPECTIVE MAKES YOU BETTER //BELIEVE IN BETTER / THE EVOLUTION OF CORE PRINCIPLES THAT PIONEERED AN INDUSTRY // BELIEVE IN BETTER / THE EVOLUTION OF CORE PRINCIPLES THAT PIONEERED AN INDUSTRY // TEAMWORK MAKES YOU BETTER // BELIEVE IN BETTER / THE EVOLUTION OF CORE PRINCIPLES THAT PIONEERED AN INDUSTRY // TAKING ACTION MAKES YOU BETTER // BELIEVE IN BETTER / THE EVOLUTION OF CORE PRINCIPLES THAT PIONEERED AN INDUSTRY // TRANSPARENCY MAKES YOU BETTER // BELIEVE IN BETTER / THE EVOLUTION OF CORE PRINCIPLES THAT PIONEERED AN INDUSTRY // DRIVING PROFITABILITY MAKES YOU BETTER // THE EVOLUTION OF CORE PRINCIPLES THAT PIONEERED AN INDUSTRY // PROCESS MAKES YOU BETTER // BELIEVE IN BETTER / THE EVOLUTION OF CORE PRINCIPLES THAT PIONEERED AN INDUSTRY // CHANGE MAKES YOU BETTER // BELIEVE IN BETTER / THE EVOLUTION OF CORE PRINCIPLE

BELIEVE IN BETTER / THE EVOLUTION OF CORE PRINCIPLES THAT PIONEERED AN INDUSTRY // AUTHENTICITY MAKES YOU BETTER // BELIEVE IN BETTER / THE EVOLUTION OF CORE PRINCIPLES THAT PIONEERED AN INDUSTRY // HUSTLING MAKES YOU BETTER // BELIEVE IN BETTER / THE EVOLUTION OF CORE PRINCIPLES THAT PIONEERED AN INDUSTRY // BELIEVE IN BETTER / THE EVOLUTION OF CORE PRINCIPLES THAT PIONEERED AN INDUSTRY // SELLING MAKES YOU BETTER // BELIEVE IN BETTER / THE EVOLUTION OF CORE PRINCIPLES THAT PIONEERED AN INDUSTRY // BELIEVE IN BETTER / THE EVOLUTION OF CORE PRINCIPLES THAT PIONEERED AN INDUSTRY // BELIEVE IN BETTER / THE EVOLUTION OF CORE PRINCIPLES THAT PIONEERED AN INDUSTRY // BELIEVE IN BETTER / THE EVOLUTION OF CORE PRINCIPLES THAT PIONEERED AN INDUSTRY // UNDERSTANDING PERSPECTIVE MAKES YOU BETTER //BELIEVE IN BETTER / THE EVOLUTION OF CORE PRINCIPLES THAT PIONEERED AN INDUSTRY // BELIEVE IN BETTER / THE EVOLUTION OF CORE PRINCIPLES THAT PIONEERED AN INDUSTRY // TEAMWORK MAKES YOU BETTER // BELIEVE IN BETTER / THE EVOLUTION OF CORE PRINCIPLES THAT PIONEERED AN INDUSTRY // TAKING ACTION MAKES YOU BETTER // BELIEVE IN BETTER / THE EVOLUTION OF CORE PRINCIPLES THAT PIONEERED AN INDUSTRY // TRANSPARENCY MAKES YOU BETTER // BELIEVE IN BETTER / THE EVOLUTION OF CORE PRINCIPLES THAT PIONEERED AN INDUSTRY // PROFITABILITY MAKES YOU BETTER // THE EVOLUTION OF CORE PRINCIPLES THAT PIONEERED AN INDUSTRY // **PROCESS MAKES YOU BETTER** // BELIEVE IN BETTER / THE EVOLUTION OF CORE PRINCIPLES THAT PIONEERED AN INDUSTRY // CHANGE MAKES YOU BETTER // BELIEVE IN BETTER / THE EVOLUTION OF CORE PRINCIPLE

Process Makes
You Better

*If you can't describe what you are doing as a
process, you don't know what you're doing.*

—W. EDWARDS DEMING

Until my time at IBM, I hadn't thought of myself as a process guy.

Looking back at my early sales days, I found that I had always been entwined in systems. Every night, I'd meticulously plan out the routes for the next day, crafting my own methods to handle my sales calls efficiently. These were the early buds of my process-focused mindset, sprouting long before the term *process* became part of my vocabulary in 2011.

Consider the case of a customer user group I established while at IBM. Unbeknownst to them, I constructed a platform for customers to exchange best practices. I encouraged organized communication through newsletters. I even orchestrated an event at the NASCAR

Hall of Fame where customers could mingle and share ideas (which, for those who know me, is the only way I'd even get near the NASCAR Hall of Fame outside of a tech conference full of IT people). This innovative approach was my way to stimulate demand without resorting to tired, old sales tactics.

You see, effective leaders know the path to success isn't always a highway. Sometimes, it's a crowded Independence Boulevard with four lanes, occasionally six, and you might encounter a flat tire on your way to the main event. But the journey to success in business isn't about the flat tire or the near-death experience while replacing it. It's about persisting, enduring, and maintaining an unwavering dedication to the process.

It's about persisting, enduring, and maintaining an unwavering dedication to the process.

As I grew my business, I was met with an onslaught of tasks and bottlenecks that made me feel like I was drowning. Dealing with claims, coordinating with field resources, confirming appointments, and collecting payments—each process brought its own unique challenges. Rather than crumbling under the pressure, I recorded every step, breaking them down into manageable tasks. This helped me find opportunities to employ specialized labor and automate certain procedures, eventually giving rise to new job titles.

This careful analysis and automation of processes led to significant profits, enough to draw the attention of private equity groups. They often wondered if my numbers were off given our unusually high profits.

By that point, I had integrated the process narrative so deeply into my company's DNA that it had become a language in its own right. Every step, every phase was represented by a number. Employees talked about being promoted to the "twos" or the "fours." This numbers game wasn't just a quirky tradition; it represented how processes had revolutionized the way we operated.

To succeed in business, leaders need to embrace the process. It might seem daunting and tiresome at first, but you need to see it as an investment that will pay out incredible dividends in the long run. With a clear, orderly process, you can accommodate customer requests for customization and handle changes without plunging the system into chaos. Your employees will keep doing their jobs, and the technology will take care of the customizations.

What most up-and-coming entrepreneurs fail to understand is that billionaires aren't made overnight. It's a painstaking, meticulous process requiring patience, an understanding of the bigger picture, and a staunch commitment to the process. As I often say, "Process prints billionaires."

But just as valuable as the profitability—maybe even more—is the sanity that process provides.

Process Provides Sanity

Early in my entrepreneurial journey, the chaos was unbearable, and everything hinged on my direct involvement. My business swung between $300,000 and $800,000 in revenue, and I had a skeleton crew of three or four employees, each one being yanked in various directions to keep things afloat. In the back of my mind, a realization began to solidify in me—process.

I remember watching companies lumber along, hitting their $5 million or $10 million mark, all while the gears of their operations gnashed against the weight of inefficiency. They understood they had to implement a process to break through to double digits, to reach that coveted "billionaire concept": a business that can scale, grow, and flourish. Even at my humble $350,000 revenue, I recognized that I needed the same thing.

Introducing a systematic process can be intimidating for many business leaders. For me, the initial stage was about confronting that fear and understanding the value of a methodical approach. It's like stepping into a dark room with a single flashlight. You have no clue what's out there, but having a consistent, steady light guiding you grants you the sanity to continue moving forward.

Think about it this way—in the absence of a process, how can you tell if you're making mistakes, let alone learning from them? Relying solely on intuition or gut feel doesn't cut it. Process allows for measurement, for tangible benchmarks that can assess whether you're on the right track. It's about realizing that making a mistake and learning from it are far better than repeating the same mistake unknowingly.

Not to mention, process empowers businesses to deliver consistently, no matter the challenge. It gives businesses like McDonald's the capacity to offer the same customer experience, the same Big Mac, whether in Paris, France, or Boise, Idaho. Process enables you to keep your promise to your customers, delivering consistent outcomes, no matter the location or circumstance.

But what happens when there's no process? Madness. The kind of chaos I've witnessed at some very large consulting firms over my career has been eye-opening. The absence of process has been glaring in mergers, consulting groups adjacent to buy side/sell side deals, technology implementations, and countless other examples with some of the world's largest companies—names you would know. The result? Unnecessary pressure, a frenzied pace of work, and always the unsettling question: "What do I do next?"

The lack of a simple Customer Relationship Management (CRM) system—a tool to keep track of where each opportunity was at any given time—just underscored this madness. It symbolized the massive inefficiencies that stemmed from a lack of process. The solution? Simply deciding to structure things systematically to mitigate the chaos.

Introducing a process is not just about bringing a sense of sanity; it's about efficiency, growth, and reliability. It's about shifting from firefighting and dealing with inefficiencies to streamlining operations and delivering consistent outcomes. Remember, as a business leader, you don't just make decisions—you build systems. And when you do, you empower your business to reach new heights.

> **Introducing a process isn't just a Band-Aid solution for immediate chaos. It's the pathway to scaling your business.**

So once you've started to master the art of process and the chaos subsides, what comes next?

As a leader, you need to take a step back and survey the landscape of your business. You're not just looking for incremental improvements anymore; you're looking for opportunities to elevate your business to an entirely new plateau. Introducing a process isn't just a Band-Aid solution for immediate chaos; it's a strategic move, a stepping stone toward something more substantial. It's the pathway to scaling your business.

Process Enables Scaling

Have you ever seen a lion tamer in action? Animal rights issues aside, it's jaw-dropping to watch such a powerful beast yield to the careful

153

management of its trainer. Imagine attempting to tame the lion without a chair, a whip, or a cage. Needless to say, it wouldn't end well for the lion tamer. As frightening as that might be, managing the beast of business is far more intimidating in my opinion.

Moving from our mauled lion tamer back to our soup analogy, I might be able to go from memory how many carrots and celery stalks I need each week. But once I start serving hundreds, or even thousands of customers, I better have processes in place to ensure I order my ingredients in advance. I need to know the exact quantity of supplies required and precisely when to place orders to keep my operations running smoothly. The same principle applies to business operations. As your business expands, the dependence on process becomes ever more vital.

Process isn't just about maintaining order or keeping things neat—it's about enhancing efficiency and throughput. A well-crafted process allows me to amplify the output of my team, thus driving profitability.

Processes aren't chains of micromanagement; they are the keys to scaling.

Not to mention, by capturing that extra profit and sharing it with my team, I can establish a virtuous cycle of motivation and productivity.

Processes aren't chains of micromanagement; they are the keys to scaling. They foster a high throughput environment that enables everyone in the organization to accomplish more. They provide clarity, align everyone's understanding, and ensure everyone is on the same page.

Processes allow your teams to go home with a sense of accomplishment and gratification, because with process they knew exactly what they needed to do that day, and when completed, they know that they had a great day at work. If you have a great day at work, you can have a great night at home with your family. Find a way to these processes together, and illustrate how it helps the company achieve the strategic plan, and you've made yourself an enterprise.

And by the way, what's wrong with micromanagement of the transactional details if your teams have a sense of fulfillment knowing that their efforts clearly impact the strategic growth and sustainability of the company? Micromanagement isn't about the people—it's about the process that drives success!

Once the process is documented, it morphs into a blueprint—a map that uncovers your business's capacity. It highlights bottlenecks, gaps, and opportunities for growth, offering you the clarity to make strategic decisions.

The process of documentation enabled me to construct the structure of my organization. It permitted me to clearly define roles and responsibilities, create job titles, and hire the right individuals to fill those roles. My processes essentially became the DNA of my enterprise, spawning a successful organization built from the inside out.

Imagine process as the scaffolding that bolsters your organization's growth. It's not just about extinguishing fires or managing chaos. It's about erecting a framework that lets you scale efficiently and sustainably.

But once the process is in place and functioning effectively, what comes next? For some, what comes next is rest, peace, and happiness in hobbies and true passions outside of business. Not for my team, however. For us, we find peace in constant improvement.

You need to find ways to consistently amplify the performance of your processes, pushing the boundaries of efficiency and productivity. This brings us to the next vital stage in your journey to have process make you better—automation.

Making Better Decisions

Imagine yourself attempting to solve an ever-changing puzzle, like a Rubik's Cube with LED lights that changes colors randomly. Pretty frustrating, right? That visual sums up the scenario I faced when my business operated without solid processes in place. Each problem solved was just a precursor to another one reappearing, trapping my team in an endless loop of issues. From my experience, this cycle inevitably leads to bottlenecks, burnouts, and a considerable waste of resources.

By systematizing the way we work, we can create more time to indulge in activities we enjoy.

Here's the thing—even if you're not aiming to scale up, perhaps running a "lifestyle business" focused more on sustaining a comfortable operation than explosive growth, processes can greatly influence your work-life balance. By systematizing the way we work, we can create more time to indulge in activities we enjoy, whether it's serving customers or fishing for bluegill on Tuesdays.

So, how exactly does process improve decision-making? This is where we transition from discussing the tangible aspects of process to the more analytical side. A well-implemented process generates consistent, structured data. This data drives your business's story, shedding light on facets of your operation that would otherwise remain hidden. This clear insight empowers us to transition from subjective to objective decision-making. It allows us to pull up the scoreboard and evaluate performance without personal biases.

I once had an employee who, despite being a little high-maintenance, was responsible for managing $2.5 million in revenue. Data provided the objective truth, enabling me to appreciate her substantial contribution while also addressing her minor disruptive impact to the team by addressing her manager with a resounding "Deal with it!"

Establishing processes provides this level of clarity across the board, enabling informed decisions that serve the entire enterprise. It can be tempting to make choices based on gut feelings or personal preferences. But the best decisions for the company often diverge from what we might instinctively choose. With a process-driven approach, decisions are grounded in data, ensuring choices are made with the company's best interests in mind.

This focus on data doesn't mean your company should lose its soul. The objective data frees you from emotional decision-making and all-nighters, tossing and turning while stressing about decision-making. It's not the only answer, but it is a very valuable one when it comes to forming a foundation for the decision criteria.

It's absolutely vital to maintain a strong, people-focused culture while sticking to rigorous processes. The transparency that process brings can be an effective equalizer, objectively evaluating performance and ensuring everyone, even friends and family within the business, is treated fairly.

Establishing processes provides this level of clarity across the board, enabling informed decisions that serve the entire enterprise.

In addition, when employees can see their performance data, they can self-manage to a certain extent, reducing the need for detailed task supervision. This shift allows leaders like myself more time to truly manage people—supporting our teams, fostering personal growth, and shaping future career paths.

In essence, building and fine-tuning your processes can morph your organization into a smoothly functioning machine. It enables you to detach from the daily minutiae and focus on guiding the ship, making decisions that benefit the entire enterprise. Process doesn't necessitate losing touch with the human side of your business. It's about creating an environment where everyone understands their roles, their performance, and their trajectory. It's about making better decisions, for your business and your people.

Only then you can effectively shift your attention to another critical aspect of business operations—customization.

Customizing the Process

Customization can be a tricky variable in the well-structured equation of process. Imagine having a well-oiled machine running flawlessly, and then a customer wants something slightly different. How do you weave that into your process without causing disruption or delays?

Let me paint a picture for you. Imagine a car assembly line. You've painstakingly built the perfect car, meticulously placing every part and considering every detail. But then, just as the car nears the end of the assembly line, a customer presents a unique request: "I'd like to buy a hundred cars, but none should have cup holders—I don't want any food in my cars because I have kids." Suddenly, you're in a predicament. You've just installed the cup holders, and now, to satisfy this customer's request, you need to remove them. Or give them some lessons in basic child-rearing techniques.

At first glance, this seems like a waste of time and materials. But there's a critical lesson I've learned as a leader: sometimes, preserving the integrity of your process demands additional efforts. To elaborate, if we take the cup holders out of the assembly line, a few things are jacked, professionally speaking.

First, the employees whom we build management teams around to recruit, hire, have a legal team for HR issues, have performance incentive plans to motivate for extra-good cup holding installation, buy hot dogs for at the picnic (or Clase Azul at the holiday party), and so on are not doing anything. Now this is only with significant scale, but in a big factory, every moment is captured, in a way that even I can't comprehend. This creates an expense that is not accurately budgeted, therefore crushing your margin, which has an impact on future pricing and the ability to compete in the future.

Second, your customers are driving your strategy, as you are reactive to the "loudest voice" syndrome. The client who has the biggest personality and loudest voice over the phone is in power—with good intentions—to get what they want, which makes them buy more but not necessarily for the greater good.

The happy ending? In the world of InsurTech, a well-thought-out healthy data architecture allows you to enable customer requests from those in power at the insurance carrier, or democratically, if someone in power does not exist, *without* disrupting the assembly line. The assembly line runs, and at the end of data aggregation and conclusions, the approved customer change orders are delivered, without (or with) the Big Gulp cup holder as witnessed in *Dumb and Dumber*.

The crux is not to disrupt the assembly line, not to upset the equilibrium of your well-established process. It's about showing respect for the process because once you don't, the entire operation is at risk of falling apart.

In business, when a request for customization arises, the initial step is to determine whether the request is applicable and beneficial to your operation. This evaluation requires a profound understanding of who's making the request and how it fits into the broader picture. Ask yourself: How many people in similar roles to this individual could potentially order our product? What's the opinion of the other nine out of ten people about this request? What does their supervisor think? This perspective allows you to better understand the demand and helps avoid impulsive decisions that could potentially derail your process.

If the request turns out to be valid and significant—such as a procurement manager at a major client asking for something different—it's time to listen. But remember, the integrity of your process is paramount. Let's say your process runs from one to ten. If a customer requests "less" of your product because of some internal restriction, you might still need to run through your entire process before adjusting the output to match the request. This might sound inefficient, but it is this kind of discipline and respect for the process that will keep your assembly line humming and your business on track.

It's about showing respect for the process because once you don't, the entire operation is at risk of falling apart.

The bottom line here is that it's critical not to allow customization requests to undermine your process or compromise the accountability of your sales team. Your team should understand the value of the process you've established and uphold it.

Take McDonald's, for instance. If a customer walked in and asked for a slice of pizza, they'd be politely informed that McDonald's doesn't serve pizza. This boils down to understanding your core offerings, adhering to them, and not getting distracted by requests that deviate significantly from what you provide.

A well-founded process enables you to cultivate a performance culture, fostering higher throughput, competitive edge, and superior customer service. It helps standardize operations, rendering metrics less subjective and more quantifiable. As the wise Peter Drucker said, "What gets measured gets managed." So, when dealing with customization requests, remember this: respect your process, measure your performance, and manage your resources efficiently.

A Fairy Tale about Process

Once upon a time, in a far-off kingdom of Industry, there lived a young and ambitious blacksmith named Eamon. Eamon's blacksmith shop was renowned across the kingdom for his magnificent tools and weapons, all thanks to his secret magic—his unique and meticulous process.

Eamon's process was nothing short of enchanting. Each step was performed with precision, the sequence was flawlessly followed, the heat of the forge was perfectly maintained, and the materials were always of the highest quality. The process was his spell, and his anvil was his wand. He used it to create unparalleled wonders that dazzled the kingdom, making him the most sought-after blacksmith in all of Industry.

Word of his magical process reached the ears of the capricious King Midas, known for his obsession with all things gold. Intrigued by Eamon's reputation, King Midas summoned him to the palace. He demanded that Eamon create a golden chariot, unrivaled in splendor, using his magical process. But there was a catch: the king, greedy as ever, insisted that Eamon should do it using less gold than was needed.

Eamon was skeptical. His process was magic, but it relied on precise quantities, the right materials, and no shortcuts. He thought about voicing his concerns to the king but decided he didn't want to offend him.

Left with no choice, Eamon returned to his blacksmith shop, wracking his brain for a way to fulfill the king's request without violating the integrity of his process. His mind buzzed with ideas, but none seemed to fit. Could his process truly be magical enough to make this possible?

After much deliberation, he had an idea. Instead of forging the chariot entirely from gold, he decided to create a golden lattice overlay on a sturdy iron frame. It would require less gold but still give the appearance of a completely golden chariot. Eamon went to work, altering his process along the way.

Finally, after days of labor, Eamon presented the golden chariot to King Midas. It was spectacular—a masterpiece that gleamed under the sun, a work of undeniable splendor. Yet, despite its magnificent appearance, it had only used a fraction of the gold a fully golden chariot would require.

King Midas, overjoyed with the result, failed to notice the underlying iron framework. He rewarded Eamon generously and paraded the golden chariot through the kingdom, showing off his newfound treasure. However, as weeks passed, the king's golden chariot started to lose its luster. The gold began to tarnish, and the underlying iron, exposed to the elements, started to rust.

King Midas was furious and summoned Eamon. Eamon explained that the request deviated too much from his proven process, and Eamon had done his best to accommodate. The issues with the chariot were an unavoidable result of trying to circumvent the process.

King Midas nodded and smiled. "Now I understand. But guess what? It's too fucking late," he told Eamon. "I, too, have a process. One for dealing with inept worms."

The guards strapped Eamon to a dolly and painfully plucked out every single hair on his head with a golden tweezer—including eyebrows, eyelashes, and his full beard. Then they covered his head in honey, wheeled him over to the giant royal ant farm on display nearby, and stuffed his head within the glass walls. While the ants did their thing, King Midas ordered Eamon's hairy back be slathered in honey from Goldilocks Ltd. honey business, while the former owners of Three Bears, Inc. nibbled every follicle off. Let's just say the bears, still pissed about their previous business failure, nibbled more than hairs from Eamon that fateful day.

Needless to say, Eamon was forced to learn a hard lesson while the king watched intently, checking each stage of his torture process off the list as it was executed. A few hours later, a headless Eamon was dipped in gold and affixed as a statue in the royal art gallery, with a plaque that read, Respect the Process.

While process can indeed seem like magic, it's not invincible. It has its principles and limits. When respected and followed, it can produce fantastic results, but when manipulated for short-term gain, it can lead to disappointing outcomes.

Reflections Make You Better

While a strong process might seem like magic, it's truly a result of diligence, precision, consistency, and respect for the principles that hold it together. When implemented and managed correctly, a process can indeed make you better in business. Here are some key takeaways on how process can significantly enhance business performance:

- **Processes Enhance Efficiency:** Well-defined processes streamline operations, minimize waste, and promote consistency. They can lead to significant time and cost savings, allowing businesses to deliver products or services faster and more efficiently.
- **Quality Control:** Standardized processes ensure that quality standards are maintained throughout the business. They help prevent mistakes and discrepancies, leading to a better customer experience and fostering a reputation for reliability and excellence.

- **Clear Expectations:** When everyone in the organization understands the process, it sets clear expectations. Employees know exactly what they need to do, reducing confusion and enhancing productivity.
- **Scalability and Growth:** Processes provide a blueprint for success that can be replicated across different teams, departments, or even geographical locations. This makes scaling your operations much easier, providing a clear path for growth.
- **Process Is Resilient:** A well-defined process can withstand changes, fluctuations in market conditions, and even internal organizational changes. It serves as a resilient backbone to your business operations.
- **Data-Driven Improvements:** Processes create measurable data, allowing for continuous feedback and improvement. What gets measured gets managed, leading to a cycle of continuous improvement and optimization.
- **Processes Promote Accountability:** When tasks and responsibilities are clearly defined within a process, it promotes accountability among team members. It becomes easier to track performance and identify any issues or bottlenecks.
- **Customizing with Care:** Processes can and should be adapted to meet customer needs but not at the expense of their integrity. Careful evaluation and thoughtful customization can enhance value without disrupting the process's overall effectiveness.

BELIEVE IN BETTER / THE EVOLUTION OF CORE PRINCIPLES THAT PIONEERED AN INDUSTRY // AUTHENTICITY MAKES YOU BETTER // BELIEVE IN BETTER / THE EVOLUTION OF CORE PRINCIPLES THAT PIONEERED AN INDUSTRY // HUSTLING MAKES YOU BETTER // BELIEVE IN BETTER / THE EVOLUTION OF CORE PRINCIPLES THAT PIONEERED AN INDUSTRY // BELIEVE IN BETTER / THE EVOLUTION OF CORE PRINCIPLES THAT PIONEERED AN INDUSTRY // SELLING MAKES YOU BETTER // BELIEVE IN BETTER / THE EVOLUTION OF CORE PRINCIPLES THAT PIONEERED AN INDUSTRY // BELIEVE IN BETTER / THE EVOLUTION OF CORE PRINCIPLES THAT PIONEERED AN INDUSTRY // BELIEVE IN BETTER / THE EVOLUTION OF CORE PRINCIPLES THAT PIONEERED AN INDUSTRY // BELIEVE IN BETTER / THE EVOLUTION OF CORE PRINCIPLES THAT PIONEERED AN INDUSTRY // UNDERSTANDING PERSPECTIVE MAKES YOU BETTER //BELIEVE IN BETTER / THE EVOLUTION OF CORE PRINCIPLES THAT PIONEERED AN INDUSTRY // BELIEVE IN BETTER / THE EVOLUTION OF CORE PRINCIPLES THAT PIONEERED AN INDUSTRY // TEAMWORK MAKES YOU BETTER // BELIEVE IN BETTER / THE EVOLUTION OF CORE PRINCIPLES THAT PIONEERED AN INDUSTRY // TAKING ACTION MAKES YOU BETTER // BELIEVE IN BETTER / THE EVOLUTION OF CORE PRINCIPLES THAT PIONEERED AN INDUSTRY // TRANSPARENCY MAKES YOU BETTER // BELIEVE IN BETTER / THE EVOLUTION OF CORE PRINCIPLES THAT PIONEERED AN INDUSTRY // DRIVING PROFITABILITY MAKES YOU BETTER // THE EVOLUTION OF CORE PRINCIPLES THAT PIONEERED AN INDUSTRY // PROCESS MAKES YOU BETTER // BELIEVE IN BETTER / THE EVOLUTION OF CORE PRINCIPLES THAT PIONEERED AN INDUSTRY // CHANGE MAKES YOU BETTER // BELIEVE IN BETTER / THE EVOLUTION OF CORE PRINCIPLE

BELIEVE IN BETTER / THE EVOLUTION OF CORE PRINCIPLES THAT PIONEERED AN INDUSTRY // AUTHENTICITY MAKES YOU BETTER // BELIEVE IN BETTER / THE EVOLUTION OF CORE PRINCIPLES THAT PIONEERED AN INDUSTRY // HUSTLING MAKES YOU BETTER // BELIEVE IN BETTER / THE EVOLUTION OF CORE PRINCIPLES THAT PIONEERED AN INDUSTRY // BELIEVE IN BETTER / THE EVOLUTION OF CORE PRINCIPLES THAT PIONEERED AN INDUSTRY // SELLING MAKES YOU BETTER // BELIEVE IN BETTER / THE EVOLUTION OF CORE PRINCIPLES THAT PIONEERED AN INDUSTRY // BELIEVE IN BETTER / THE EVOLUTION OF CORE PRINCIPLES THAT PIONEERED AN INDUSTRY // BELIEVE IN BETTER / THE EVOLUTION OF CORE PRINCIPLES THAT PIONEERED AN INDUSTRY // BELIEVE IN BETTER / THE EVOLUTION OF CORE PRINCIPLES THAT PIONEERED AN INDUSTRY // UNDERSTANDING PERSPECTIVE MAKES YOU BETTER //BELIEVE IN BETTER / THE EVOLUTION OF CORE PRINCIPLES THAT PIONEERED AN INDUSTRY // BELIEVE IN BETTER / THE EVOLUTION OF CORE PRINCIPLES THAT PIONEERED AN INDUSTRY // TEAMWORK MAKES YOU BETTER // BELIEVE IN BETTER / THE EVOLUTION OF CORE PRINCIPLES THAT PIONEERED AN INDUSTRY // TAKING ACTION MAKES YOU BETTER // BELIEVE IN BETTER / THE EVOLUTION OF CORE PRINCIPLES THAT PIONEERED AN INDUSTRY // TRANSPARENCY MAKES YOU BETTER // BELIEVE IN BETTER / THE EVOLUTION OF CORE PRINCIPLES THAT PIONEERED AN INDUSTRY // PROFITABILITY MAKES YOU BETTER // THE EVOLUTION OF CORE PRINCIPLES THAT PIONEERED AN INDUSTRY // PROCESS MAKES YOU BETTER // BELIEVE IN BETTER / THE EVOLUTION OF CORE PRINCIPLES THAT PIONEERED AN INDUSTRY // **CHANGE MAKES YOU BETTER** // BELIEVE IN BETTER / THE EVOLUTION OF CORE PRINCIPLE

Change Makes You Better

Change before you have to.

—JACK WELCH

Take a moment, and think about the word *change*. What images does it conjure up? Some might immediately think of dirty diapers, as a breakfast conversation with my wife revealed. Go ahead and laugh, but there is a profundity to those dirty diapers—they underscore that current perspective matters. Your personal understanding and reaction to change will significantly shape how you navigate it.

Your personal understanding and reaction to change will significantly shape how you navigate it.

In business and in life, change is an inexorable force. And it possesses a dual nature—fear and opportunity. To the leaders, entrepreneurs, and executives reading this, I urge you to remember: Change equals better. It's a simple, powerful formula. A better version of your organization can only arise when change has been implemented, received, and integrated into your company's culture. This philosophy is deeply embedded in Alpine Intel's own operating principles.

One pearl of wisdom I've often shared is, "Change or be changed by someone else." Sure it's harsh, but it's the key to sustainable growth. Bet the house on it, because it will happen. The moment you choose to ignore change, you set the stage for your downfall.

However, if you choose to embrace change, to see it as a catalyst for innovation and advancement, you unlock unlimited potential for your organization's development.

But let me make one thing clear: Embracing change isn't about changing for the sake of change or adopting new practices without careful consideration. It's about making strategic, data-driven decisions that align with your company's goals, mission, and vision. It's about fostering an environment where change isn't feared but welcomed.

As business leaders, it's essential to remember that the pursuit of stability must not undermine the pursuit of growth.

When things become too predictable, too comfortable, that's when the danger seeps in. For me, stability in business can become a slippery slope toward stagnation, which is the beginning of the end. As business leaders, it's essential to remember that the pursuit of stability must not undermine the pursuit of growth.

In spite of that very long pearl necklace of various wisdom, I need to acknowledge that some individuals thrive in stability. Nothing wrong with that. We're all wired differently. But in the dynamic landscape of business, change is the unseen catalyst for growth.

Embrace it, leverage it, and watch your organization ascend to unprecedented heights. *You* are the master of your fate. *You* hold the reins to your business. Are you ready to believe in better? Are you ready to believe in change?

As deep as we're about to go into the ocean of change, it's imperative not to lose sight of your destination. Just like a ship navigating the vast ocean, you need to leverage the winds of change in business without allowing them to pull you off course. So how do you make sure to stay on course?

Vision.

Vision—the Core of Leadership

Let's imagine a manager as a gardener, engrossed in the details of the here and now. The manager has their hands in the soil, pruning, planting, weeding, and spreading manure (figure of speech). Their attention is anchored to the moment, engaged in the constant maintenance that makes their garden thrive *today*.

A leader, however, embodies the visionary landscaper, looking out into the horizon. They envision the landscape *tomorrow*—five years down the line when the saplings have matured into towering trees, when the blooming flowers have painted the scenery with a splash of vibrant colors. The leader is not just responding to the present but also sculpting the future.

The core of leadership is vision—the capacity to see beyond the present, to envisage the future, and to navigate those seas of change between the two—also known as the strategic vision. It's a common misconception that change always implies a drastic alteration in the strategic vision of a company. Change can just as well be about narrowing your focus, about fortifying what your company does best, about resisting the allure of shiny new ventures that pull you off course.

Did you know, when you hop on your favorite commercial airline, slip into that neck pillow you always swear to wash when you get home but never do, and wait for the beverage cart to come by so you can get your Stroup waffle, that for a considerable portion of the flight the airplane is off course? With the aid of autopilot or the constant vigilance of the pilots themselves, the airplane makes continuous course corrections to make sure you reach your destination on time. The same applies to leaders and business. They face the daunting task of steering the company through both calm waters and tumultuous storms, making small tweaks to keep the journey aligned with their strategic vision.

Great leaders never change for the sake of change. Instead, they leverage their entrepreneurial intuition, the innate sense telling them when something doesn't quite fit with the strategic vision. They are always several moves ahead even while working toward the current goal.

We'll get into what exactly drives change a little later in the chapter. But it almost always occurs in one of two forms: offensive change and defensive change.

Defensive Change

In case you weren't aware, change doesn't just sneak up on you while you're sipping your morning coffee. In business, change is like a street fight—it's raw and relentless, and if you don't fight back, you're going to end up face down on the pavement with a mouthful of broken teeth.

With our own development, we didn't just choose the shiny, exciting changes to go after. We rolled up our sleeves and dove face first into the hard, tedious parts of our development architecture—the bits that let us be dynamic, nimble, and flexible when the time comes to change. Not just changing for the sake of changing, following some new business fad. Defensive changes are about making a conscious, strategic decision to change—based on the trends, not because of them.

Imagine you just got promoted from the captain of the ship in the previous example to a Navy admiral at the helm of an aircraft carrier turning the ship into a submarine because submarines are the thing in naval warfare. Absurd? Hell yes. But that's what leaders end up doing to their company when they just jump onto every bandwagon that passes without really considering their strengths, vision, and strategy.

As a leader, I've found that everyone seems to have an opinion on what creates our value. One day it's all about ROI. The next it's how we're going to be displaced by artificial intelligence (AI) and ChatGPT. I mean, remember when everyone was scrambling about crypto? This is where defensive change comes in. It's about understanding, not just reacting.

Yes, ChatGPT and AI are disruptive forces, and they're here to stay. But rather than running around like a chicken with its head cut off, why not take a moment to understand what's really going on?

In my humble opinion, ChatGPT, at the time of this writing, is like a supercharged search engine. It aggregates data, but that doesn't mean it's always right or will provide a consistent solution. But we

This is where defensive change comes in. It's about understanding, not just reacting.

can use it to gather information more rapidly than ever before. Sounds boring? Maybe. But sometimes, it's not about inventing a brand-new business model. It's about building faster, more efficiently, leveraging the tools at hand. That's the overlooked beauty of change.

The essence of defensive change is like a good game of chess. You keep your eye on the board; you anticipate your opponent's moves; you guard your king. But remember this: change is about not forgetting what got you to the game in the first place. It's about using that as your foundation while you adapt, grow, and innovate. You never want to lose your identity in the face of change or transform your business just for the sake of it. That's not change; that's surrendering.

Offensive Change

Offensive change. This phrase alone paints a picture of a forceful, assertive strategy—making bold moves and setting the pace rather than merely reacting. And while offensive change can sometimes be, well, offensive, it's often the key to unlocking new levels of success for your organization. It's about taking the initiative, whether that's tackling internal issues head-on or being bold enough to redefine your strategic direction.

Consider my company's development team for instance. Here was a situation where a crucial component of the business was hindering growth, essentially becoming an internal obstacle. Recognizing this issue, I didn't hold back. I decided to expand the development team by an astounding 150 percent, bringing on new employees and taking risks along the way. The result? Four years later, around 90 percent of those hired are still con-

That's the essence of offensive change, confronting problems head-on and initiating proactive transformations that lead to long-term benefits.

tributing to the organization's success. That's the essence of offensive change, confronting problems head-on and initiating proactive transformations that lead to long-term benefits.

It's a tough lesson, but as a leader, you need to make the hard decision to let go of people who are holding the organization back, even if it's the entire development team or half of the sales force. This is offensive change in action: it's assertive, it's forward-thinking, and, most important, it prioritizes the company's growth over maintaining the status quo.

However, let's not forget that change can also be driven by external influences, some of which can be less than helpful. I've experienced situations where shareholders and external voices try to steer the organization in a direction that might not align with my strategic vision. They might argue for changes in the business model, insist on following the latest industry trends, or even suggest sacrificing our hard-earned intellectual capital.

When confronted with these pressures, it's crucial to remember the purpose of change. It should be to add value, not just to appease external pressures. So, how do you decide when to listen and when to forge your own path? As leaders, we need to assess the proposed changes, ask critical questions, and discern whether the suggestions align with the organization's strategy and vision.

One method I recommend is assigning "homework" to gauge the validity of an idea. If the person suggesting the change is truly invested in it, they'll have no issue digging deeper, answering your questions, and substantiating their proposal.

In essence, offensive change, whether it's internal or driven by external pressures, should serve one primary purpose: adding value to your organization. It should move you closer to your strategic vision, not detract from it. Any change that doesn't add value or align with your vision is merely a distraction, no matter how loud the voices advocating for it are.

Remember, change isn't just about reaction; it's about forward motion, it's about strategic transformation, and most important, it's about ensuring that every step you take moves you closer to your goal.

So now for the million-dollar question: How do you know when it's the right time to instigate change?

Knowing When to Change

Unfortunately, there is no magic formula or one-size-fits-all answer. Knowing when to embrace change is less of a science and more of an art, I'll admit. It's like a Van Gogh—a little messy, a bit unpredictable, but in the end, it's stunning.

Whenever I come across a potential change, I put it through a rigorous test, kind of like a drill sergeant at boot camp. Does it positively impact our value to the customer? Does it enhance our product delivery? Does it keep our employees, from the front line to the executive suite, engaged and excited about the future? This process helps me weed out the changes that align with our core values and business objectives.

As our organization grew, I added a new layer to this test, something I like to call an "obligation to understand." It recognizes that great ideas can come from the outside. But it's not about blindly accepting these ideas; it's about discerning whether they fit our overall business strategy. It is the obligation of the executive and management teams to seek to understand. This is the only way to validate and influence change.

One time, we considered expanding our HVAC consulting model to include a repair arm, a classic case of "getting high on our own supply" (a tip of the hat to The Notorious B.I.G. there). While the idea seemed lucrative, it didn't align with our business model and introduced more risk and responsibility than we were willing to shoulder.

In another instance, there was an internal push to develop software for our competitors and insurance companies. I quickly shot this down, as it felt like willingly giving up our competitive advantage—kind of like a boxer showing his opponent how to throw the perfect punch.

Take our transition to "Alpine," for another example. Names and labels do not matter as much as principles and operating fundamentals. We made sure that the change resonated with our core values and direction. Even in the choice of the new name, "Alpine," we held on to the spirit of continuous growth, always looking to scale the next peak.

Knowing when to change is just as critical as knowing what changes to make.

Knowing when to change is just as critical as knowing what changes to make. Changes should benefit the company, its customers, its employees, and its future. They should align with your core values and propel you toward your goals, not lead you astray. Be open to change, sure, but also be discerning. Ideas are a dime a dozen; making the decisions is real value.

Understanding when and what to change is a delicate dance, a balance between your business acumen, your understanding of your organization, and your eye for the right opportunities.

A Fairy Tale about Change

Once upon a time, in a lush forest full of businesses run by all manner of creatures, there lived a diligent ant named Anthony and a laid-back caterpillar named Carl. Each ran their own little business—Anthony managed a bustling food storage enterprise, while Carl ran a cozy leaf-eating establishment.

Now, Anthony was known throughout the forest for his commitment to change. He was always seeking ways to improve, be it a more efficient method of storing food or better ways to serve his fellow forest creatures. He had this uncanny knack for turning every setback into an opportunity, a trait that earned him the respect of his peers.

Carl, however, believed in the old ways. "Why fix what isn't broken?" he would often ask. His business thrived on a steady diet of leaves, and he saw no reason to change a winning formula.

One day, a rumor started floating around the forest. Whispers of a coming frost that would wipe out the lush vegetation, rendering the forest bare. Anthony heard this and immediately saw the need for change. He convened a meeting with his team, and they decided to diversify, to store not just food but also materials to help keep their fellow creatures warm during the frost.

Carl heard the rumor too, but he brushed it off. "It's been cold before. Why stress?" he scoffed, continuing to munch on his leaves, confident that his leaf-eating business would remain unaffected.

Frost arrived sooner than expected, turning the lush forest into a barren, icy landscape. Leaves became scarce, and Carl's business suffered. He was forced to turn his forest friends and longtime customers away empty-handed. His complacency had cost him dearly, and he found himself on the brink of bankruptcy. He created a small cocoon for himself and shut himself inside to ride it out.

Meanwhile, Anthony's business was booming. His decision to diversify had paid off. His fellow creatures now depended on him not just for food but also for warmth. His business became the backbone of the forest's economy, ensuring the survival of its inhabitants during the harsh winter.

As spring returned and the forest sprung back to life, Carl finally emerged from his cocoon, now transformed into a beautiful butterfly. But his business had collapsed. He flew over to Anthony, humbled and in awe of the ant's foresight.

In his complacency, Carl had overlooked the most crucial lesson in business—change is inevitable, and adapting to it is key. Meanwhile, Anthony, the ever-agile ant, had understood that embracing change was not about discarding the old but about innovating and growing better.

Carl now understood, and he was ready to change. He fluttered around the rejuvenated forest, deciding to start a new venture, one that would use his newfound ability to fly, catering to the transport needs of smaller creatures. But it was too fucking late.

The forest creatures who had depended on Carl were pissed— those who survived the frost, that is. They had been forced to scavenge for food, and sadly, many of them perished from hunger. A group of rhinoceros beetles captured Carl in a net, while a family of roly-polies ripped off his beautiful wings. As Carl squirmed in the dirt, a praying mantis swept him up and hopped up a tall Birch tree, feeding Carl's body to a Great Horned Owl who lived on a branch high above.

The last thing to go through Carl's mind as he passed into the owl's beak, wriggling and wailing, was this: change means nothing if the timing is off.

Reflections Make You Better

By embracing change and viewing it as an ally rather than an obstacle, you can unlock new possibilities, stay ahead of the curve, and continuously evolve your business for greater success. Here are some key takeaways on how change makes your business better:

- **Embrace Change as a Catalyst for Growth:** Change is not something to fear but rather an opportunity to grow and improve. It opens doors to new ideas, strategies, and perspectives that can propel your business forward.

- **Adaptability Is Key:** In a rapidly evolving business landscape, adaptability is crucial. Being open to change allows you to stay ahead of the curve, meet customer needs, and seize emerging opportunities.

- **Continuous Innovation Drives Success:** Innovation is the lifeblood of business success. Embracing change fosters a culture of innovation, enabling you to develop new products, services, and processes that keep you relevant and competitive.

- **Don't Fear Failure:** Change often comes with risks, and setbacks may occur along the way. However, failure is an essential part of the learning process. Embrace it as an opportunity for growth, refine your approach, and keep pushing forward.

- **Challenge the Status Quo:** By questioning existing practices and seeking new solutions, you can challenge the status quo within your industry. Breakthroughs happen when you dare to challenge conventional wisdom and explore uncharted territory.

- **Stay Customer-Centric:** Change allows you to better understand and serve your customers. By adapting to their evolving needs and preferences, you can build stronger relationships, enhance customer satisfaction, and drive loyalty.

- **Foster a Culture of Change:** Change is not a one-time event but an ongoing process. Encourage your team to embrace change and be proactive in seeking opportunities for improvement. Cultivate a culture that values continuous learning, adaptability, and resilience.

- **Balance Consistency and Innovation:** While change is important, it's also essential to maintain consistency in your core values and brand identity. Find the right balance between preserving what makes your business successful and embracing innovation.

- **Seek Feedback and Collaboration:** Engage with your team, customers, and stakeholders to gain valuable insights and perspectives. Actively seek feedback, collaborate with others, and be open to their ideas. Together, you can drive positive change and achieve greater success.

- **Personal Growth Drives Business Growth:** Finally, remember that change isn't just about business outcomes but personal growth as well. Embrace change as an opportunity to learn, develop new skills, and become a better leader. Your personal growth will ultimately contribute to the growth and success of your business.

BELIEVE IN BETTER / THE EVOLUTION OF CORE PRINCIPLES THAT PIONEERED AN INDUSTRY // AUTHENTICITY MAKES YOU BETTER // BELIEVE IN BETTER / THE EVOLUTION OF CORE PRINCIPLES THAT PIONEERED AN INDUSTRY // HUSTLING MAKES YOU BETTER // BELIEVE IN BETTER / THE EVOLUTION OF CORE PRINCIPLES THAT PIONEERED AN INDUSTRY // BELIEVE IN BETTER / THE EVOLUTION OF CORE PRINCIPLES THAT PIONEERED AN INDUSTRY // SELLING MAKES YOU BETTER // BELIEVE IN BETTER / THE EVOLUTION OF CORE PRINCIPLES THAT PIONEERED AN INDUSTRY // BELIEVE IN BETTER / THE EVOLUTION OF CORE PRINCIPLES THAT PIONEERED AN INDUSTRY // BELIEVE IN BETTER / THE EVOLUTION OF CORE PRINCIPLES THAT PIONEERED AN INDUSTRY // BELIEVE IN BETTER / THE EVOLUTION OF CORE PRINCIPLES THAT PIONEERED AN INDUSTRY // UNDERSTANDING PERSPECTIVE MAKES YOU BETTER //BELIEVE IN BETTER / THE EVOLUTION OF CORE PRINCIPLES THAT PIONEERED AN INDUSTRY // BELIEVE IN BETTER / THE EVOLUTION OF CORE PRINCIPLES THAT PIONEERED AN INDUSTRY // TEAMWORK MAKES YOU BETTER // BELIEVE IN BETTER / THE EVOLUTION OF CORE PRINCIPLES THAT PIONEERED AN INDUSTRY // TAKING ACTION MAKES YOU BETTER // BELIEVE IN BETTER / THE EVOLUTION OF CORE PRINCIPLES THAT PIONEERED AN INDUSTRY // TRANSPARENCY MAKES YOU BETTER // BELIEVE IN BETTER / THE EVOLUTION OF CORE PRINCIPLES THAT PIONEERED AN INDUSTRY // DRIVING PROFITABILITY MAKES YOU BETTER // THE EVOLUTION OF CORE PRINCIPLES THAT PIONEERED AN INDUSTRY // PROCESS MAKES YOU BETTER // BELIEVE IN BETTER / THE EVOLUTION OF CORE PRINCIPLES THAT PIONEERED AN INDUSTRY // CHANGE MAKES YOU BETTER // BELIEVE IN BETTER / THE EVOLUTION OF CORE PRINCIPLE

Conclusion

Every ending is a beginning. We just don't know it at the time.

—MITCH ALBOM

The book is done, but you're still here, which means you definitely believe in better, because you are always on the lookout for more.

We covered the top ten things that I've found make you better—a better leader, a better business, a better human being. Are there more? Sure. We didn't even get to topics like creativity, leadership, adversity, or discipline. Will I write about them someday? Perhaps.

But, since you're here, you might as well read another story. This one, in particular, encapsulates every lesson from this book in a single scenario. It actually qualifies as the worst meeting of my entire life.

It all started on a snowy Sunday night in Connecticut. A close colleague and I had spent weeks prepping and *hustling* as we boarded a flight from Charlotte to Hartford for what I thought would be a routine sales call to nail one of our largest clients at that time, a global insurance firm. Why Sunday during a snowstorm, you ask? We wondered the exact same thing. The company had called the meeting for Monday morning at the bell, and they showed no sign of rescheduling. Of course, we were high-fiving, because the signal for getting a new client doesn't get any better than that. But even if we were able to touch down in Hartford safely, we still didn't know if we would be able to drive our rental car to the meeting in near-blizzard conditions. Sure, we could have done a call or Skype from the comfort of North Carolina, but as you'll recall, my team strives for *authenticity*. And there is no better way to express authenticity than to be in person, especially when the stakes are high.

The next morning, I was dressed in my sport coat and crisp white shirt, ready to take on the world. We started strong, using plays from chapters like *selling* and *teamwork* to keep the momentum. And then, just when we thought everything was going swimmingly, the head of claims morphed into our worst nightmare. The whole time we were presenting, he had remained quiet, attentive. But now he was making oddball requests, such as asking to see the résumés for our top talent and members of our executive leadership team. I suddenly realized what was happening. One of my former business partners had recruited an A player from the person whom we were trying to close a deal with, and this guy was still seething while taking the personnel loss personally. We had been set up! That's why he made us leave home on a Sunday night and didn't cancel despite the blizzard! Revenge well played, sir!

The tone of the meeting instantly transformed. I felt like I was in the Spanish Inquisition as he laid into me. My colleague couldn't do anything to assist. Talk about having to navigate our ship through tumultuous waters. But here's where things took a turn. While accusations flew and tensions peaked, I found my center and somehow remained calm—despite the fact that my blood pressure was off the charts. Responding with respect, I championed our company and its employees. I didn't back down, but I also didn't take the bait from this ass clown. Through *taking action* and showcasing *transparency*, I tried to steer the conversation back on course, clarifying the definition of partnership, and in this case, we weren't being treated like a partner—we were simply a vendor to him.

The meeting eventually ended on a super awkward note. I don't know, maybe it was the fact that he had sixteen of his senior managers around the country, who represented millions of revenue, on a conference call the whole time, telling them they weren't allowed to do business with us unless he personally approved it. Needless to say, we left thinking we lost the deal of a lifetime. Then I decided to embrace the head of claims' *perspective*. The individual we hired was indeed exceptional, and his former employer was frustrated we recruited him. The irony is this employee we inadvertently recruited was worth more than the revenue represented in this room—and on the conference call, though we didn't know that at the time. The decision to recruit him was made by others in my company, but I wrote the head of claims a sincere letter and owned it. I never received a personal response, but when we wheeled back around about our companies doing business together, the energy had changed, and we were able to ink a massive deal.

The thing is, this tale isn't just about one turbulent meeting; it's a testament to how I've tried to incorporate every chapter of this book into my life. When facing challenges, I always aim for *profitability*. Embracing *change*, I endeavored to better myself and the company. And despite grappling with hurdles that could've easily shaken my resolve, I was all about the *process*, prioritizing the company and its people.

Life has taught me to *believe in better*—always. So, as you flip these last pages, realize it's more than words—it's a journey. And if you are still reading, you're probably thinking there might be another fairy tale.

OK, but this is the *last one*.

In the enchanting land of Literaria, nestled deep within the Forest of Fables, stood a grand library. This library was home to every story ever written and those yet to be inked. Within its walls resided a particular book that was whispered about by every reader, known as *The Infinite Chronicle*.

The Infinite Chronicle wasn't like other books. It was kept atop the highest tower in the library, a staggering 7,245 feet in the air. Very few had ever made the long journey up the winding staircase but those who had reported what they saw. A single room with stone floors and walls, and in the center was a pedestal with a grand book bound in white buffalo skin and cured in Buffalo Trace, with silver pages. Inscribed in the pedestal was the following riddle: *For those who believe in better, a tale continues ever after. The key is in naming the author.* Every page could be read and turned save one—the last one.

The contents of the book were said to be life changing for those who had the pleasure of reading it. And each person said the same thing after making the long, arduous climb down the staircase: "Praise be, I didn't want it to end!" But end it did, for those who couldn't decipher the riddle.

Year after year, readers tried and failed to decipher the riddle. Some sought to turn the page forcibly, others whispered spells, while a few sang enchanting melodies. But the page remained steadfast.

Then, one day, a young entrepreneur named Gary visited the library. He lived in a far-off land and heard rumors of *The Infinite Chronicle*, the impossible riddle, and the difficult trip to the top of the tower. He had an idea, one that would make the wisdom in the book available to all. Gary would embark on the long climb to the top of the tower, record every word in the book, reprint it under his name, and share it with the entire realm for ten bucks a pop, since not everyone could make such a difficult trip.

Step-by-step, he climbed each of the 7,245 risers in the staircase, shouting unearthly curses at every single one. Once at the top, he was in awe of the magnificence of the book resting on the pedestal. He carefully read and copied each word onto parchment he had brought along, marveling at the silvery pages. He could even see his reflection through the words! When he finally reached the final page, like all the others, he didn't want it to end. It was simply a blank silver page, reflecting back his expression of woe. He tried to turn it, but it wouldn't budge.

Suddenly, he thought about the words of the riddle: *For those who believe in better, a tale continues ever after. The key is in naming the author.*

Looking into his reflection, he realized the riddle's answer. The last page wasn't a page at all. It was a mirror. "The author of the next chapter is ... *me!*"

Of all people, Gary had solved the riddle. But it was too fucking late. What Gary failed to spot at the beginning of the book was the copyright symbol. And by transcribing each word onto parchment with the intent to make a profit, he had violated one of the library's most ancient laws, punishable by such agony that death was preferable. Invisible hands grabbed Gary fiercely and slammed him to the stone floor. Then he was thrust, head first, down the staircase, his face bashing into each of the 7,245 steps.

By the time he reached the bottom, he no longer looked like Gary the entrepreneur. His face resembled a bloody pile of scalloped potatoes, sprinkled with nutmeg. In a daze he wandered through the village, trying to cry for help, but he lost most of his teeth between steps 6,578 and 6,109. And his tongue fell out on step 3,314. The townspeople decried the hideous monster and chased him into a small barrel, which they set aflame and rolled down the mountain-side. Miraculously, Gary survived the fall, though he was eaten by a mountain lion shortly after.

The moral? The next chapter is yours to write.

ELIEVE IN BETTER / THE EVOLUTION OF CORE PRINCIPLES THAT PIONEERED AN INDUSTRY // AUTHENTICITY MAKES OU BETTER // BELIEVE IN BETTER / THE EVOLUTION OF CORE PRINCIPLES THAT PIONEERED AN INDUSTRY // HUSTLING MAKES YOU BETTER // BELIEVE IN BETTER / THE EVOLUTION OF CORE PRINCIPLES THAT PIONEERED AN INDUSTRY // BELIEVE IN BETTER / THE EVOLUTION OF CORE PRINCIPLES THAT PIONEERED AN INDUSTRY // SELLING MAKES YOU BETTER // BELIEVE IN BETTER / THE EVOLUTION OF CORE PRINCIPLES THAT PIONEERED AN INDUSTRY // BELIEVE IN BETTER / THE EVOLUTION OF CORE PRINCIPLES THAT PIONEERED AN INDUSTRY // BELIEVE IN BETTER / THE EVOLUTION OF CORE PRINCIPLES THAT PIONEERED AN INDUSTRY // BELIEVE IN BETTER / THE EVOLUTION OF CORE PRINCIPLES THAT PIONEERED AN INDUSTRY // UNDERSTANDING PERSPECTIVE MAKES YOU BETTER //BELIEVE IN BETTER / THE EVOLUTION OF CORE PRINCIPLES THAT PIONEERED AN INDUSTRY // BELIEVE IN BETTER / THE EVOLUTION OF CORE PRINCIPLES THAT PIONEERED AN INDUSTRY // TEAMWORK MAKES YOU BETTER // BELIEVE IN BETTER / THE EVOLUTION OF CORE PRINCIPLES THAT PIONEERED AN INDUSTRY // TAKING ACTION MAKES YOU BETTER // BELIEVE IN BETTER / THE EVOLUTION OF CORE PRINCIPLES THAT PIONEERED AN INDUSTRY // TRANSPARENCY MAKES YOU BETTER // BELIEVE IN BETTER / THE EVOLUTION OF CORE PRINCIPLES THAT PIONEERED AN INDUSTRY // DRIVING PROFITABILITY MAKES YOU BETTER // THE EVOLUTION OF CORE PRINCIPLES THAT PIONEERED AN INDUSTRY // PROCESS MAKES YOU BETTER // BELIEVE IN BETTER / THE EVOLUTION OF CORE PRINCIPLES THAT PIONEERED AN INDUSTRY // CHANGE MAKES YOU BETTER // BELIEVE IN BETTER / THE EVOLUTION OF CORE PRINCIPLE

BELIEVE IN BETTER / THE EVOLUTION OF CORE PRINCIPLE
THAT PIONEERED AN INDUSTRY // AUTHENTICITY MAKES
YOU BETTER // BELIEVE IN BETTER / THE EVOLUTION
OF CORE PRINCIPLES THAT PIONEERED AN INDUSTRY //
HUSTLING MAKES YOU BETTER // BELIEVE IN BETTER /
THE EVOLUTION OF CORE PRINCIPLES THAT PIONEERED AN
INDUSTRY // BELIEVE IN BETTER / THE EVOLUTION OF CORE
PRINCIPLES THAT PIONEERED AN INDUSTRY // SELLING
MAKES YOU BETTER // BELIEVE IN BETTER / THE EVOLUTION
OF CORE PRINCIPLES THAT PIONEERED AN INDUSTRY //
BELIEVE IN BETTER / THE EVOLUTION OF CORE PRINCIPLES
THAT PIONEERED AN INDUSTRY // BELIEVE IN BETTER /
THE EVOLUTION OF CORE PRINCIPLES THAT PIONEERED AN
INDUSTRY // BELIEVE IN BETTER / THE EVOLUTION OF CORE
PRINCIPLES THAT PIONEERED AN INDUSTRY // UNDERSTANDING
PERSPECTIVE MAKES YOU BETTER //BELIEVE IN BETTER /
THE EVOLUTION OF CORE PRINCIPLES THAT PIONEERED AN
INDUSTRY // BELIEVE IN BETTER / THE EVOLUTION OF CORE
PRINCIPLES THAT PIONEERED AN INDUSTRY // TEAMWORK
MAKES YOU BETTER // BELIEVE IN BETTER / THE EVOLUTION
OF CORE PRINCIPLES THAT PIONEERED AN INDUSTRY //
TAKING ACTION MAKES YOU BETTER // BELIEVE IN BETTER
/ THE EVOLUTION OF CORE PRINCIPLES THAT PIONEERED AN
INDUSTRY // TRANSPARENCY MAKES YOU BETTER // BELIEVE
IN BETTER / THE EVOLUTION OF CORE PRINCIPLES THAT
PIONEERED AN INDUSTRY // DRIVING PROFITABILITY MAKES
YOU BETTER // THE EVOLUTION OF CORE PRINCIPLES THAT
PIONEERED AN INDUSTRY // PROCESS MAKES YOU BETTER //
BELIEVE IN BETTER / THE EVOLUTION OF CORE PRINCIPLES
THAT PIONEERED AN INDUSTRY // CHANGE MAKES YOU BETTER
// BELIEVE IN BETTER / THE EVOLUTION OF CORE PRINCIPLE